THE REDE
OF THE
WICCAE

Adriana Porter, Gwen Thompson, and the Birth of a Tradition of Witchcraft

Robert Mathiesen
and
Theitic

Olympian Press
Providence, Rhode Island

Olympian Press
P. O. Box 29182
Providence, RI 02909

ISBN 0-9709013-2-1 - Softcover
ISBN 0-9709013-1-3 - Hardcover

Printing   5 4 3 2 1   Year   09 08 07 06 05

Printed in the United States of America.

Cover design by Olympian Press. Book design and typesetting by Aardvark Graphics.

Dedication

This book is dedicated to the memory of Adriana (1857-1946) and Gwen (1928-1986) and to all families who have preserved their hidden wisdom from generation unto generation and kept their secret fires burning.

Contents

Acknowledgments

Robert and Theitic wish to acknowledge the support and encouragement that they have received from the N.E.C.T.W. Council of Elders in all their efforts to shed more light on the origins and early history of Lady Gwen Thompson's Tradition of the Craft.

Robert also wishes to thank his wife, Theresa Elva Mathiesen, for all the time and care that she took in repeatedly proofreading and editing successive drafts of this book, and his undergraduate research assistant, Michelle Menard, who helped greatly with the final proofreading. Any remaining errors are, of course, his fault, not theirs.

We also wish to thank Vicki DiOrazio for her creativity and the numerous design improvements which have contributed so much to this work.

In addition we would like to thank Ogmios for his artistic contribution and for his countless hours of photo restoration.

Lastly, we wish to thank Lenura without whose administrative and communicative help the project could not have come into being.

Preface

This book attempts to critically examine one of the Craft's well-known grandmother tales. This is the tale told by Gwen (later Gwynne) Thompson about her grandmother, Adriana Porter, and how she came to be the last carrier of her ancestral Tradition of Witchcraft. Gwen herself published very few words on the subject in 1975, but she told her initiates much more than she published and gave to them a large book of texts that she said had come to her from her grandmother. The contents of this book are oath-bound and restricted to initiates in the Tradition that she founded and a few other Traditions closely associated with it. Gwen wrote that her Tradition's "public name" for this book was the *Book of Shadows*—implying that her initiates know it under some other secret name.* We shall simply call it her *Book*.

The work contained herein is the result of an unusual collaboration. The senior collaborator (Robert) never met Gwen Thompson. He is not an initiate in her Tradition of Witchcraft or any Tradition associated with hers, and he is not familiar with the contents of Gwen's *Book*. He is a medieval philologist who has had a life-long interest in the history of magical practices and doctrines and alternative religions. He has been a professor at Brown University since 1967, where he now teaches courses on the above-mentioned subjects. The junior collaborator (Theitic) met Gwen Thompson in the year 1974 and studied with her until 1978, and remained in touch with her on and off until her death in 1986. Since 1978 he has been an Elder in the Tradition that she founded, and he is now its historian and archivist. Robert and Theitic have been friends for more than 10 years now.

The text of this work was mostly organized and written by Robert, who is also responsible for the historical background and genealogical data on which it depends. Theitic is responsible for the information about Gwen Thompson herself, her life and her immediate family, and about the Tradition of Witchcraft that she founded. Robert and Theitic share responsibility for the conclusions, which are the product of many hours of discussion.

Robert and Theitic share the hope that their collaboration may serve to illustrate one way in which scholarly research can be conducted responsibly when much of the relevant evidence is oath-bound, and thus is not available to all the collaborators alike, and cannot be cited or published, but only described in extremely general terms. It requires an uncommon level of mutual trust and respect for two people to collaborate as scholars under such a condition. Robert, however, is confident that his trust in Theitic (and the Council of Elders of Gwen Thompson's Tradition of the

---

*Lady Gwen. "Wiccan-Pagan Potpourri," *Green Egg* 69 (Ostara 1975): 9-11 (quote on p. 10), reprinted in Appendix E.

Craft) has not been misplaced, and he feels himself honored by the trust that they in turn have reposed in him.

They also share a two-fold hope for the future. First, they hope that other teams of initiated elders and uninitiated professional scholars will work together to study the history of other Traditions of Witchcraft and Paganism in much the same manner, and to publish objective and rigorous studies for the uninitiated public, whether academic or not. Second, they hope that their work will inspire at least a few initiates who are also professional academics to carry out rigorous scholarly investigations of the history of their own Traditions on the basis of all evidence available to them as initiates, and to document the results of their work for circulation only among their fellow initiates. Even though such work remains as oath-bound as the evidence on which it rests, it will inevitably lead to greater self-knowledge within each Tradition. Wise indeed were the words once carved above the doorway to the temple at Delphi.

ΓΝΩΘΙ ΣΕΑΥΤΟΝ
Know thyself!

The present work is offered as a modest response to that Delphic command.

Introduction

Around the year 1950 there emerged from the shadows a new religious movement of considerable staying power and significance. This religion took for itself the ancient name of Witchcraft, but is now more widely known as Wicca.

The early growth and spread of Witchcraft as a religion owed much to the efforts of the redoubtable Gerald Brosseau Gardener (1884-1964).[1] This self-educated man was the author of two obscure historical novels about Witches, *A Goddess Arrives* (1939) and *High Magic's Aid* (1949), as well as two quasianthropological books, *Witchcraft Today* (1954) and *The Meaning of Witchcraft* (1959). The religion that he popularized in these works was both magical and initiatory. He presented it as an ancient Pagan religion that had been driven underground by the spread of Christianity. It had been nearly exterminated during the Great Witch Hunt in the sixteenth and seventeenth centuries, but had survived as the secret practice of a few families and covens.

As Gardner told the story of his own discovery of Witchcraft, he had long suspected that a significant fraction of the many women and men executed for maleficium (i.e., sorcery or witchcraft) during the fifteenth, sixteenth, and seventeenth centuries had in fact been secret adherents of a pre-Christian religion that had died out long before the twentieth century. But in 1939, when Gardner was initiated into a small group of men and women with strong occult interests, he discovered "that that which I had thought burnt out hundreds of years ago still survived"—the Old Religion of the Witches still lived.[1]

For about 10 years Gardner seems not to have made much use of his new knowledge of Witchcraft. These were, after all, the years of the Second World War and its aftermath. Around 1950, however, he began very quietly to initiate a few people as Witches and to create a coven of his own. In 1951 he first appeared in public as a Witch. Newspapers took note, and the ensuing publicity brought many people to him who wished to become Witches. Because several doctrines and practices of this religion meshed very well with the dominant cultural themes of the sixties and seventies, the number of initiated Witches rose sharply. By 1970 there was no turning back.

Gardner's initiates received from him not only oral teaching, but also a collection of writings that he called the *Book of Shadows*. Despite its title, this *Book of Shadows* was not a book in the sense of a volume that had a fixed text and a definite table of contents. Rather, it was a loose collection of separate writings, that had as its principal parts about two dozen prose texts on magic and ritual practice and on the governance of covens, eight rites for the eight major feasts (Sabbats) of the turning year, rituals of initiation into three degrees of the Craft, and about one dozen texts on other elements of ritual practice, such as Casting and Closing the Circle, Consecrating the Working Tools, the Charge of the Goddess, Drawing Down the Moon, and the Great Rite. Some of these writings are several pages long, others only a few lines. Individual copies of the *Book of Shadows* differed in the order in which these writings appeared, and also in the selection of texts which were included therein. There was also considerable variation in the actual words of some of the included texts. By now, 50 or more years later, individual copies of the *Book of Shadows* very often have come to include many texts composed since Gardner's time. Also, many Witches who are not linked to Gardner by any chain of initiations use the title for their own collections of secret or sacred texts.

Although the texts and rituals in Gardner's *Book of Shadows* seem to be quite old at a first reading, closer analysis reveals that many of them contain quotations from the works of such men as Charles G. Leland, S. L. MacGregor Mathers, Aleister Crowley, and Oliver Bland—as well as Mark Twain and Rudyard Kipling.[2] These particular texts, of course, cannot be older than the publications from which they quote. Such an analysis proves conclusively that Gardner's *Book of Shadows* cannot have assumed its final form much before about 1930, though of course some parts of it may be a little older.

During the 1960s and 1970s other people came forward claiming to be Witches who owed little or nothing to Gardner and his works. Among them were Charles Cardell (Rex Nemorensis), Sybil Leek, Roy Bowers (Robert Cochrane), Alex Sanders, and Jessie Wicker Bell (Lady Sheba), to name just a few of the most prominent. Some of them, in particular Alex Sanders and Lady Sheba, transmitted the texts in Gardner's own *Book of Shadows* (as well as other texts) to their own initiates, claiming that their versions of these texts were independent of Gardner's. (However, it is now clear that these claims were false.[3]) Others, notably Robert Cochrane, denied the authenticity of Gardner's Witchcraft altogether.

Because of all this, the 1960s and 1970s were the time of the "grandmother tales."[4] These are stories that were told by many people in support of their independent authority as Witches. Typically the Witch who told a grandmother tale claimed that a long line of her ancestors—usually her women ancestors—had been Witches, but they had kept their Witchcraft as a deep family secret. The last of those Witch ancestors was the teller's grandmother (or rarely some other aged female relative), from whom the teller received her own teaching and initiation as a child. In some of these grandmother tales, Witchcraft had been the secret heritage of a whole family, taught to all its members. In others, it was passed on only rarely, to an exceptionally talented and promising child or grandchild. In some cases, the grandmother had not intended to pass her Witchcraft on to anyone, but had been forced to do so by the teller's own chance discovery of the family secrets. In all cases, the grandmother herself is now dead, so the tale must be taken on trust.

Virtually all grandmother tales end by telling how the family's Witchcraft, which had been kept as a treasured secret for uncounted generations, was now at risk of being lost forever. Sometimes this was because the teller had no children and grandchildren of her own; sometimes because the younger generation was too modern to care about such an old-fashioned thing as Witchcraft. In any event, the teller has come to a crossroads. Shall she keep her family's rule of secrecy and allow the ancient secrets to die with her? Or shall she break it and teach them to outsiders?

Most of these grandmother tales do not hold up well under critical examination. (In a few cases the teller eventually admitted that her tale was the product of wishful thinking and youthful enthusiasm.) As professional historians and folklorists began to look at the grandmother tales, scholarly criticism of them became more cogent and well-founded. A few recent books have made the Wiccan community very much aware of this critique and how persuasive it is. As a result, many Wiccans have come to discount all grandmother tales without exception. Even Gerald Gardner's account of how he met his own initiators has been rejected by some as a falsehood, though it is not the usual sort of grandmother tale at all. For quite some time now, many Wiccans have preferred to claim that their religion is a revival, not a survival. (Thus they have also felt free to invent and reinvent their religion in any way that speaks to their own lives and needs.)

Yet it is a mistake (and an error in scholarly method) to dismiss every grandmother tale out-of-hand as a complete fabrication. Philip Heselton has now found and published significant evidence to support Gardner's own claim that a group of occultists initiated him around 1939, telling him that they practiced Witchcraft or Wica (Gardner's spelling of Wicca). Heselton has even discovered the identity of some of these occultists and Witches.[5] Gardner's initiators, of course, may have told him that their traditions were centuries old. If they did so, then he accepted their claims uncritically, since they fitted his preconceptions so well.

In this case the important question is not simply whether Gardner embellished the truth, or even told downright lies. Gardner himself says that Witches are "consummate leg-pullers" and the witness of people who knew him amply confirms that Gardner himself was fond of pulling people's legs even about Witchcraft.[6] Rather, the question is how one may best distinguish between the plain truth and its embellishments within the tales that Gardner told. Heselton has already found several kernels of truth in Gardner's tales, and he hopes to find more as he continues patiently to examine each and every small detail in the light of all available sources of information. Heselton is fully aware how complicated a task this is. Not only must one remove the embellishments and falsifications to uncover what Gardner actually believed was the truth, but then one must test each such belief to see whether Gardner himself may have been mistaken, or even deceived by others. The task is not an easy one.

Endnotes

1. Bracelin, J. L, and Gerald Gardner. *Witch.* London: Octagon Press, 1960, p. 165.

2. Most of these sources were first identified in print by Aidan A. Kelly, *Crafting the Art of Magic, Book I: A History of Modern Witchcraft, 1939-1964* (St. Paul, Minn.: Llewellyn, 1991); but see also his *Inventing Witchcraft: The Origins and Nature of Gardnerian Neopagan Witchcraft as a New Religion* (unpublished work, 1988). The quotation from Mark Twain's *A Connecticut Yankee in King Arthur's Court,* chapter 28, was first noticed by "Pagan X," "A Connecticut Yankee in King Arthur's Coven," *Enchanté: The Journal for the Urbane Pagan* 10 (Brumalia 1991), p. 25. It occurs in the text "Of the Ordeal of the Art Magical," which was not included by Kelly in *Inventing Witchcraft* (at least in the 1988 text available to me), but printed in *Crafting,* p. 88-89. Although Kelly rightly notes that it occurs in Gardner's manuscript, "Ye Bok of ye Art Magical," nevertheless he took this text not from that source, but from Janet and Stewart Farrar, "A Witches Bible Compleat." New York: *Magickal Childe,* II (1984): 57. The text "To Gain the Sight," Kelly, *Crafting,* p. 91-94; also Farrar and Farrar, "A Witches Bible Compleat," p. 58-9; quotes from Oliver Bland's book, *The Adventures of a Modern Occultist.* New York: Dodd, Mead and Co., 1920, p. 99-100 and 122-23.

3. For Alex Sanders, see Ronald Hutton, *The Triumph of the Moon: A History of Modern Pagan Witchcraft.* Oxford: Oxford University Press, 1999, chapter 17. Copies of letters by Lady Sheba disproving her claim are in the possession of one of the Elders of N.E.C.T.W.

4. See Margot Adler, *Drawing Down the Moon: Witches, Druids, Goddess-Worshippers, and Other Pagans in America Today,* rev. ed. Boston: Beacon Press, 1986, chapter 4.

5. Philip Heselton, *Wiccan Roots: Gerald Gardner and the Modern Witchcraft Revival.* Chieveley, Berks.: Capall Bann, 2000; *Gerald Gardner: Witchcraft Revival.* Thame: I-H-O Books, 2001; *Gerald Gardner and the Cauldron on Inspiration: An Investigation into the Sources of Gardnerian Witchcraft.* Milverton, Somerset: Capall Bann, 2003.

6. Gardner, Gerald. *Witchcraft Today.* London: Rider, 1954, p. 27: "Witches are consummate leg-pullers; they are taught it as part of their stock-in-trade."

Part 1

Investigating Gwen Thompson's Grandmother Tale

Any investigation of Gwen Thompson's grandmother tale must begin with her own brief comments on the subject in an article of hers. The article, with the title "Wiccan-Pagan Potpourri," appeared in issue #69 of the magazine *Green Egg* (for Ostara 1975), pages 9-11 (see Appendix E).

In that article, Gwen Thompson characterized herself as a "Traditionalist, versed in lore taken from certain Witches of the British Isles." She also published one short text, *The Rede of the Wiccae,* from her *Book,* introducing it with the following words:

> *Our own particular form of the Wiccan Rede is that which was passed on to her heirs by Adriana Porter, who was well into her nineties when she crossed over into the Summerland in the year 1946.*

She was led to do so because another person had recently published the same text "in a perverted form," and she wished to set the record straight. [She is referring to the text of the "Rede" printed in Herman Slater's *Earth Religion News,* volume 1, issue 3 (Spring Equinox, 1974), p. 3, see Appendix E.]

Gwen Thompson's initiates heard more of the tale from her. They are willing to share the following mundane details with the uninitiated. Gwen Thompson was born Phyllis Ruth Healy on September 16, 1928. She was the only child of Walter Ellsworth Healy and Ola Blanche Turner. Her father, too, had been an only child, the son of William Henry Healy and Adriana Porter. At first these five people all lived in one house in Melrose, a town near Boston, Massachusetts, and Phyllis's mother and grandmother both took care of her when she was a child. When Phyllis was only three years old, her father died. Soon her grandfather Healy also died, leaving the three women with the house, but not much income. Thus Phyllis's mother took a job to support the family, and Phyllis was mostly raised by her grandmother.

Adriana Porter had come to Massachusetts from Yarmouth, Nova Scotia, where her family had lived for at least a few generations. She was a daughter of Henry Porter and Sarah Arnot Cook. Sarah was a daughter of John Cook and Wealthy Trash. (Trash turns out to be a dialect pronunciation of the uncommon surname Trask, which we shall use throughout this book.)

Gwen Thompson told her initiates that her grandmother's family were carriers of a secret Tradition of folk Witchcraft that had come down through Sarah Arnot Cook and Wealthy Trask (Trash) from the latter's seventeenth-century ancestors. These ancestors had come to Salem, Massachusetts, from Somerset County in England, a county famous for Witchcraft and also for secret traditions about Glastonbury, Avalon, and King Arthur.

Gwen also told her initiates that her father, Walter Healy, had been a Rosicrucian. (At least four distinct Rosicrucian orders were flourishing in the 1920s. It is not known to which of them he belonged.) Additionally, she told them that her grandmother had initiated her and her mother into the family's Tradition of Witchcraft, and had given them their Craft names. This is how Phyllis became Gwen.

As Gwen told the story, her mother remarried not long after the death of her first husband. Her new husband, Chester D. Stetson, was a conservative Protestant Christian. After her remarriage, Gwen's mother adopted her new husband's religion and broke with her first husband's occultism and his family's Tradition of Witchcraft. From that time on she kept young Gwen away from her grandmother. However, Adriana Porter remained in Melrose until her death in 1946, when Gwen was 18 years old, and Gwen continued to cherish her memories of her grandmother.

When Adriana Porter died, Gwen received an inheritance from her, which was a trunk containing family heirlooms and possessions. In this trunk she found a bundle of loose papers tied up in a faded red ribbon, which recorded her grandmother's family and its Tradition of Witchcraft. She studied these papers carefully and copied them, arranging her copies in a three-ring binder. In this way she created her own *Book* as a record of her family's Witchcraft and magic. After she had copied the original papers, she destroyed them. From time to time Gwen recopied individual pages in her *Book* as they aged and faded, or because she thought she could make them look nicer—or simply because she felt like doing so. She continued to recopy individual pages up to the end of her life. When she recopied a page, she destroyed her earlier copy.

Gwen had originally planned to keep her Tradition of Witchcraft within her own family. She married a man named John Grimes, by whom she had a daughter and a son, but this marriage ended in divorce. (She told her later initiates that she had initiated her children and her son's wife and children and given them their Craft names.) After the breakup of Gwen's first marriage, however, her son and his wife raised their children as Christians, and Gwen had relatively little contact with them. Gwen's daughter had no children. Gwen married two more times, thereby changing her married surname from Grimes to Johnson and then to Thompson, but these marriages did not last long and produced no children.

Because of these things, Gwen finally resolved to initiate outsiders, fostering them as members of her own family. Otherwise, she feared, her Tradition and her knowledge would perish with her. She first initiated a few outsiders in the late 1960s. Several years later, in 1972, she and several of her earlier initiates created a formal organization, the New England Covens of Traditionalist Witches (N.E.C.T.W.). It carefully protects and preserves her heritage today.

Some of Adriana Porter's close relatives remained in Yarmouth, while others settled elsewhere in Canada or the United States. No doubt some of them have living descendants today, whose names could be recovered from public records. Certainly Gwen visited relatives both in Yarmouth and in Rhode Island. However, she always refused to tell her initiates anything about the identity of her living relatives, saying, "They don't want to talk to you!"

Gwen Thompson died on May 22, 1986, while visiting relatives in Yarmouth. By good fortune her own *Book*—still in the form of loose pages kept in a three-ring binder—eventually came into the hands of her legitimate Craft heirs. It has been carefully preserved ever since by the N.E.C.T.W.

Our Research

Unlike the oldest parts of Gardner's *Book of Shadows*, Gwen Thompson's *Book* has never been published, but has been kept sacred and oath-bound until now. Therefore Robert has not been in a position to examine it, or to apply to its contents the source-critical methods that have successfully been used to fix the age of certain texts in Gerald Gardner's *Book of Shadows*, and that he himself has elsewhere applied to Charles Godfrey Leland's very influential work, *Aradia or the Gospel of the Witches of Italy.*[1] Even so, he has been able to pursue several lines of research to the point where they shed some new light on Gwen's claim to have inherited a family Tradition of Witchcraft.

First, by genealogical research Robert has been able to identify Adriana Porter and her immediate family more fully, and to trace her genealogy and identify the majority of her ancestors, including Sarah Arnot Cook and Wealthy Trask (Trash), back to the early 1600s. He has also been able to confirm that Wealthy Trask's ancestors indeed came from Somerset County, England, as Gwen said. To be more precise, they came from the small town of East Coker, about three miles southwest of Yeovil and about 20 miles south of Glastonbury.[2]

He has further been able to show that Adriana Porter's seventeenth-century ancestors in New England included an alchemist, Jonathan Brewster, as well as members of several of the warring families that played a large role in the Salem witch hunt of 1692, though as accusers and their opponents, not as victims. Her ancient relatives in Salem and nearby were the Trasks and Putnams on her mother's side, and the Hales and Porters on her father's.

Second, Robert has been able to show that the environment in which Adriana Porter spent her younger years was rich in traditional folklore and "superstition" (as the educated elite would have termed it). He has also been able to show that she spent her married life in places that were hot beds of esoteric, occult and magical doctrines and practices, as well as centers of unconventional spirituality and religion, during the decades when she lived there.

Thus Adriana Porter could easily have found both teachers and books to further her interest in such things, had she wished to do so. Moreover, some of these teachers laid claim to the same powers that Witches had used in the past. At least one of these teachers (Emma Hardinge Britten) was even willing to concede, now and then, that she might rightly be called a Witch, were it not for the negative overtones of that word.

Finally, Robert has closely examined the sole text from Gwen's *Book* that has been published, namely, the *Rede of the Wiccae*. His analysis has yielded certain highly suggestive results concerning the manner of its composition and the time when it first reached its present form.

The remainder of this book will present his results on each of these three subjects in turn.

Endnotes

1. Most of these sources were first identified in print by Aidan A. Kelly, *Crafting the Art of Magic, Book I: A History of Modern Witchcraft, 1939-1964* (St. Paul, Minn.: Llewellyn, 1991); but see also his *Inventing Witchcraft: The Origins and Nature of Gardnerian Neopagan Witchcraft as a New Religion* (unpublished work, 1988). See also Robert Mathiesen, "Charles G. Leland and the Witches of Italy: The Origin of Aradia," in Mario and Dina Pazzaglini, *Aradia or the Gospel of the Witches: A New Translation.* Blaine, Wash.: Phoenix Publishing, 1998, p. 25-57.

2. William Blake Trask, "The Traske Family in England," *The New England Historical and Genealogical Register* 54 (1900): p. 279-83.

The Family Tree of Adriana Porter

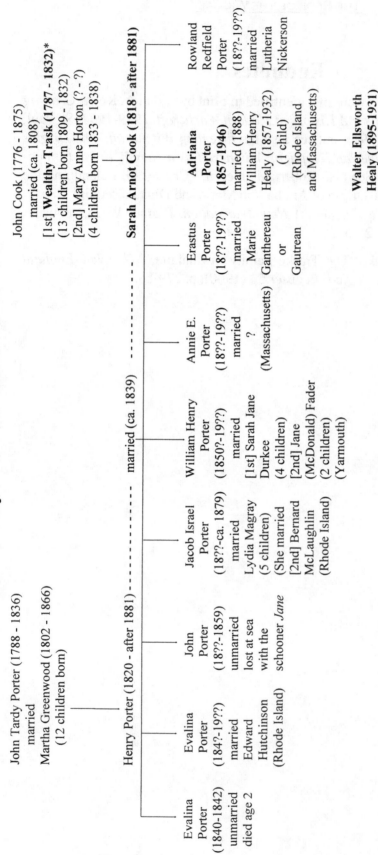

John Cook (1776 - 1875)
married (ca. 1808)
[1st] **Wealthy Trask (1787 - 1832)***
(13 children born 1809 - 1832)
[2nd] Mary Anne Horton (? - ?)
(4 children born 1833 - 1838)

John Tardy Porter (1788 - 1836)
married
Martha Greenwood (1802 - 1866)
(12 children born)

Sarah Arnot Cook (1818 – after 1881)

Henry Porter (1820 - after 1881) - - - - - - - - married (ca. 1839) - - - - - - - -

Rowland Redfield Porter (18??-19??) married Lutheria Nickerson

Adriana Porter (1857-1946) married (1888) William Henry Healy (1857-1932) (1 child) (Rhode Island and Massachusetts)

Erastus Porter (18??-19??) married Marie Ganthereau or Gautrean (Massachusetts)

Annie E. Porter (18??-19??) married ?

William Henry Porter (1850?-19??) married [1st] Sarah Jane Durkee (4 children) [2nd] Jane (McDonald) Fader (2 children) (Yarmouth)

Jacob Israel Porter (18??-ca. 1879) married Lydia Magray (5 children) (She married [2nd] Bernard McLaughlin (Rhode Island)

John Porter (18??-1859) unmarried lost at sea with the schooner *Jane*

Evalina Porter (184?-19??) married Edward Hutchinson (Rhode Island)

Evalina Porter (1840-1842) unmarried died age 2

Walter Ellsworth Healy (1895-1931) married (1925) Ola Blanche Turner (1903-1996) (She married [2nd] Chester D. Stetson)

Phyllis Ruth Healy (= Gwen Thompson) (1928-1986) (married three times) (Mass. and Conn.)

*The names in bold type are the lineage that Gwen Thompson claimed for her Tradition of Witchcraft.

Part 2

Who Was Adriana Porter?

The Course of Adriana Porter's Life

Each of the United States Federal census returns for Massachusetts in 1900, 1910, 1920, and 1930 has an entry for Adriana Porter and her family, as does the Canadian census for Nova Scotia in 1881. These five documents, together with her husband's immigration papers, and various public and private records of births, marriages, and deaths, frame the stages of Adriana Porter's life. (Transcriptions or abstracts of them can be found in Appendix D.) From them we can recover the following facts that confirm the few mundane names and dates in Gwen Thompson's grandmother tale.

Adriana Porter was born in late July 1857, at Yarmouth, Nova Scotia; no record of the exact day of her birth has yet been found. Her parents were Henry Porter and Sarah Arnot Cook, who married around 1839. Adriana was the eighth of their nine known children, who were all born between 1840 and about 1860.[1] They appear to have been born in the following order.

- Evalina (died on Dec. 31, 1842, at age 2)
- Evalina (again)
- John (died at sea in March 1859)
- Jacob Israel
- William Henry (born around 1850)
- Annie E. Erastus
- Adriana (born in 1857)
- Rowland Redfield

On page 10 the reader will see a family tree showing Adriana Porter's parents and grandparents, her siblings, and her descendants.

Note how the second daughter was given the same name, Evalina, as her older sister, who died in infancy. Until around 1800 it was very common in New England for the name of a child who had died in infancy to be given again to the next-born child of the same sex. Such recycled names are called necronyms by genealogists. Around 1800 the use of necronyms became unfashionable in New England, as the entire system for naming children changed at that time.[2] After the Revolutionary War, however, the former New Englanders who had settled in Nova Scotia tended to resist innovations from the United States. Thus they preserved the older system of naming children for a generation or two longer. Although the two Evalinas provide a good example of a necronym, Gwen Thompson told her initiates that their mother, Sarah Arnot (Cook) Porter, had named her second daughter Evalina in the firm belief that she was the first Evalina reincarnated, and she offered this as evidence for her ancestral Tradition of Witchcraft.

Adriana and William Henry Porter seem to have been the only two of these nine children who had not left Yarmouth by 1881. By that year William had already married (Sarah Jane Durkee, daughter of Freeborn Durkee) and they had four children. He and his family were living in Yarmouth, in the next house over from his parents. Adriana herself was still unmarried and living in her parents' house.

Although most of her ancestors had been men of substantial property and position in Nova Scotia, Adriana Porter and her siblings appear to have been reduced to quite modest circumstances by 1881. Henry Porter was listed in the 1881 census as a truckman, William as a common laborer, and Adriana herself as a seamstress.

Yarmouth had once been a wealthy town, one of the more prosperous seaports in Nova Scotia. Its strongest industry was the building of wooden sailing ships, and fishing ran a close second. By 1870, however, the market for wooden sailing ships had begun to collapse, as more and more iron steam ships were built and put into service. Yarmouth did not rise to this challenge very well, and by 1881 the town had clearly fallen on hard times.[3] Many of its young people, men and women alike, had already left for greener pastures—including most of Adriana Porter's brothers and sisters.

Two of her grown brothers and sisters seem to have gone to Rhode Island, namely, Jacob Israel and Evalina. There Jacob Israel Porter married Lydia Abigail Magray on August 26, 1867. Lydia, too, had been born in Nova Scotia. They had several children in Rhode Island. Evalina also married a man from Rhode Island, whose name was given by one genealogist as Edward Hutchinson.[4] This may be an error, since it has not yet been possible to identify her husband under this name, to find a record of her marriage, or to trace her life after her marriage either in the United States or in Canada.

Nor has it been possible to trace her other brothers and sisters after their marriages, although it is clear that they had all left Yarmouth by 1881. One genealogist identified Erastus's wife as Marie Gautrean or Ganthereau of Clare, Digby County, Nova Scotia, and Rowland's as Lutheria Nickerson (daughter of James Nickerson). He did not identify Annie's husband, but said that she was married in Massachusetts.[5]

Adriana Porter also eventually left Yarmouth. It appears that first she followed her brother and sister to Rhode Island, for in that state she met William Henry Healy and married him on April 24, 1888. Adriana's husband had been born in Windsor, Nova Scotia, on March 17, 1857.[6] He had immigrated from that city to Watertown, Maine, on October 15, 1878, when he was 21 years old, but later he moved to Rhode Island. Between 1888 and 1906 he and his wife appear to have moved from place to place in Massachusetts and Rhode Island, but in 1906 they settled in Melrose, Massachusetts, where they remained until their deaths.

William H. Healy was a man of several professions. In 1895 he was employed as a surveyor, in 1902 he called himself a civil engineer, and in 1900 and 1910 he was listed by the census-taker as a bookkeeper (working for a contractor in 1900, for a construction company in 1910). By 1900 he was earning enough money that his wife did not need to work. In 1918 he became an insurance broker and was able to buy his own house at 76 First Street in Melrose, Massachusetts. It was a attractive house, seemingly built in the late 1800s, perhaps the oldest house on its block. He continued to work as an insurance broker until he was struck down by a motorcycle on May 7, 1932. He died three days later, on May 10, in Central Hospital, Somerville.

Although William Healy and Adriana Porter were married for more than 40 years, they seem to have had only one child, Walter Ellsworth Healy. He was born in Plymouth on July 2, 1895, a few weeks before his mother turned 38. During the First World War, while serving in France, he was gassed. This disabled him for the rest of his life, and after 1926 he was unable to work. He lived with his parents until his death. Earlier, however, he was employed at various times as a clerk, an "electric crane man," an engineer in a leather factory, and finally as a house painter. He died at home on August 29, 1931, from the effects of wartime gas poisoning.

On April 16, 1925, when he was 29 years old, Walter Healy married Ola Blanche Turner at Melrose. She had been born in Canada on May 5, 1903. In 1921, when she was 18 years old, she immigrated to the United States. She was 21 years old when she married. Three years later, on September 16, 1928, their only child,

Phyllis Ruth, was born at Melrose. As already noted, Walter Healy died three years later, in 1931, and Adriana Porter lost her own husband, William Healy, in 1932.

According to the annual Poll Tax Lists published by the Town of Melrose and the published biennial directories of the inhabitants of Melrose, Adriana Porter Healy continued to live at 76 First Street together with Ola Turner Healy until 1941, when Phyllis was about 13 years old. By 1942 Adriana had moved into Fitch Home, a very elegant home for the elderly and infirm at 75 Lake Avenue, Melrose. Ola remained one more year at 76 First Street, but then she took lodgings at 33 Vine Street, only a few blocks from Fitch Home. Adriana died on March 1, 1946, at Fitch Home, as a result of heart disease, from which she had suffered for 25 years.

In 1945 Chester D. Stetson took lodgings at 33 Vine Street. Within a year he and Ola were married, and had moved into slightly better housing at 84 Cottage Street, Melrose, where they remained until 1947.[7]

Walter, William, and Adriana (Porter) Healy were all buried in Wyoming Cemetery, Melrose; in 1986 Phyllis's—Gwen's—ashes were also buried in the same cemetery plot (section 2 of lot 400).

Adriana Porter's Ancestry

As noted above, Adriana Porter was born at Yarmouth, Nova Scotia, in 1857. She was the eighth of nine children born to Henry Porter and Sarah Arnot Cook, who married around 1839. Fortunately, a competent local historian, George S. Brown (1827-1915), a man born and raised at Yarmouth, long ago mined the local records and the memories of living elders to work out the genealogy of many old Yarmouth families. He published his work in the columns of the *Yarmouth Herald* during the years 1896-1909, and all of his columns were republished as a book in 1993. Among the Yarmouth residents whose ancestry he documented for several generations were both of Adriana Porter's parents, Sarah Arnot Cook and Henry Porter.

As it turned out, all four of Sarah Arnot Cook's grandparents, as well as most of her great-grandparents, were already known to specialists in the history and genealogy of old New England, who had long ago traced their ancestry back to the very first settlers of that region. This also turned out to be the case for just one of Henry Porter's grandparents, namely, his father's father. (The ancestry of his father's mother has only recently been established; that of his mother's parents remains unknown.) All of the details are given in the genealogical charts in Appendix A, with full documentation. Here it will be enough to summarize the most important facts.

Sarah Arnot Cook's Ancestry

One of Sarah Arnot Cook's grandfathers, Ephraim Cook, had come to Nova Scotia from Massachusetts in 1762 in company with George Ring, whose eldest daughter, Louisa, he married in 1764. Ephraim Cook soon became one of the foremost men in Yarmouth County. He served as Registrar of Deeds in 1762, and was also a member of the small committee that laid out lands for the first settlers. In 1767 he was appointed a Justice of the Peace, and was awarded one share in the division of lands of Yarmouth Township. Both he and his father-in-law held the military rank of Captain in the militia, as did his son John, the father of Sarah Arnot Cook. The Cooks and the Rings came from the old colony of Plymouth. (Plymouth was incorporated into Massachusetts in 1691, and retained a sense of its own separate identity well into the eighteenth century.)

Sarah Arnot Cook's other grandfather, John Trask, had come with the family of his father, Elias Trask, to Nova Scotia from Massachusetts sometime between 1763 and 1766. John married Mehitable Clements at Yarmouth in 1773. She was the daughter of John Clements, an experienced and prosperous sea captain from Salem and Marblehead, and his wife, Hannah Eaton. Like his father-in-law, John Trask followed the sea, first as a member of the crew of John Clements' schooner. By 1780, however, John Trask had acquired his own ship, "a small boat of about eight tons." Both the Trasks and the Clements were originally from Salem. The Eatons, like the Cooks and the Rings, were originally from Plymouth Colony.

Many of Sarah Arnot Cook's earliest Plymouth ancestors—for whatever the fact may be worth—had arrived on the ship *Mayflower* in 1620.[8] These ancestors ranged in social position from William Brewster, who was the first Teaching Elder of Plymouth Church, to John Billington, who was the first man hanged for murder in Plymouth (in 1630). They also included Mary Chilton, who was an irrepressible girl of 13 when the *Mayflower* landed and who somehow managed to be the very first European female to set foot on Plymouth Rock (or wherever it was that the passengers first stepped onto the beach at Plymouth)—a tale which she delighted to tell until her dying day.[9]

Sarah Arnot Cook's earliest Salem ancestor was William Trask. He was one of the very first men to settle at Salem, arriving in 1624 aboard the ship *Zouche Paris,* six years before the so-called "Great Immigration" of Puritans in 1630. He had been born in East Coker, Somerset County, in 1585. In old Salem he prospered, acquiring much land and wealth.

Most of William Trask's children and grandchildren remained at Salem, but one of his grandsons, also named William Trask, left the area and moved to Weymouth, Massachusetts, around 1700. Alone of all the Trasks, this younger

15

William was linked by close ties of kinship to Thomas Putnam Jr. and his wife Ann Carr, the chief instigators of the famous witchcraft trials. Indeed, his mother was Thomas Putnam's sister Ann, so he was also a first cousin to Ann Putnam Jr., the most forward of the teen-aged "afflicted girls" whose testimony ruined so many lives in 1692.

After the hysteria had ended, much opprobrium seems to have been heaped upon the Putnams' heads. In 1699 Thomas Putnam died at the age of 46 years; his wife died 15 days later, when she was just 37 years old. Historians have speculated lightly about their deaths as two suicides or a murder and a suicide. Their daughter Ann appears never to have married. For many generations thereafter few if any Putnam girls were given the name Ann.

In view of all this scandal and opprobrium that touched his close relatives, young William Trask may well have wished to make a new life for himself away from Salem. He married and had children only after he had left Salem. One of his sons was the above-mentioned Elias Trask, the first of that name to settle in Nova Scotia.

Henry Porter's Ancestry

Henry Porter's ancestry has been traced only on his father's side; the ancestry of his mother, Martha Greenwood, remains a puzzle.

Henry Porter's father was John Tardy Porter, who was sufficiently prosperous in 1826 to commission the building of a wooden ship of 18 tons, the schooner *Fanny*. He died on October 6, 1836, probably before Henry had attained his majority. John Tardy Porter was the seventh of 14 children born to Nehemiah Porter Jr. and his wife, Mary Tardy. Mary Tardy's parents were John Tardy, a sea captain who commanded the brig *Hooper* out of Salem in the 1760s, and Ruth M. Blaney, both of Marblehead (near Salem, Massachusetts). The Tardys moved from Massachusetts to Halifax, Nova Scotia, around 1774.[10]

Nehemiah Porter Jr.'s father was Nehemiah Porter Sr., who was a Congregational minister (Harvard, class of 1745). Nehemiah Sr. had come to Yarmouth just in time to take part in the first division of the town lands (April 1767), through which he and his sons together received the very large share of 2,915 acres. In September, 1767, the first Congregational Church in Yarmouth was formed, and Nehemiah Sr. was called to be its first minister.[11] As a minister and a Harvard graduate, he ranked with Ephraim and John Cook, John Trask and John Clements in status and position, if not in wealth. However, Nehemiah Sr. returned to Massachusetts in 1771, where he served as the Congregational minister in Ashfield for some 40 years. He died in

1820, about a month before his one hundredth birthday. Of all his children, only Nehemiah Jr. remained at Yarmouth.

The ancestors of Nehemiah Porter Sr. in the male line can be traced back to John Porter, who immigrated from England to Massachusetts in 1835 and settled at Salem in 1643. The line runs through John's son Samuel, a mariner who died in Barbados, and Samuel's son John, who was the grandfather of Nehemiah Sr. John was a man in his middle thirties at the time of the Salem witch hunt. Although the Porters seem to have been deeply involved in the trials, having long opposed the Putnam family at nearly every point, they left only a few traces in the surviving court records of 1692. Indeed, no Porter was ever accused as a witch. Thus it is hard to say how large a role John and his wife Lydia Herrick played in the trials.

Nehemiah Porter Sr. had taken a wife from another family of Congregational ministers. She was a daughter of John Chipman (Harvard, class of 1711), who was the first minister in North Beverly, Massachusetts. John Chipman's wife, in turn, was a granddaughter of John Hale (Harvard, class of 1657), who had been the minister at Beverly, Massachusetts, at the time of the Salem witch hunt in 1692, and had played a role in it. Shortly after the end of the trials John Hale had become conscious of his mistakes in judgment. This led him to write one of the more valuable and insightful books about the witchcraft trials, titled *A Modest Enquiry into the Nature of Witchcraft* (completed in 1697, published posthumously in 1702).

As a genealogical curiosity, it is worth noting that Henry Porter and Sarah Arnot Cook were fourth cousins. Each of them was a great-great-great-grandchild of Samuel Chipman and Sarah Cobb through different sons. Henry Porter was a descendant of the above-mentioned John Chipman, minister at North Beverly. Sarah Arnot Cook was a descendant of John's younger brother, Jacob Chipman. (See Appendix A.)

Religious Affiliations of Adriana Porter's Ancestors

If Adriana Porter was indeed a bearer of a secret family Tradition of Witchcraft, as Gwen Thompson claimed, then the religious affiliation of her ancestors has a certain interest.

Although people commonly think of colonial New England as a unified Puritan theocracy, the historical reality was far more complex. Only three old colonies, namely, Massachusetts Bay, Connecticut, and New Haven, were Puritan strongholds. Plymouth Colony was Separatist, Rhode Island and Providence Plantations was officially tolerant of all faiths, and the other old colonies—Saybrook, New Hampshire, and the lands that later became Maine—were more interested in trade and fishing than in religious controversy.

From their places of settlement it can be argued that only a few of Adriana Porter's seventeenth-century ancestors were Puritans. Indeed, many of them are known to have been Separatists rather than Puritans.

What distinguishes a Separatist from a Puritan? To oversimplify matters, Puritans were radical religious reformers who hoped to purify the established Church of England from centuries of corruption and superstition, working from inside. Separatists, however, were far more radical than Puritans; they thought that the Church of England had become much too corrupt to ever be purified at all, so that it was best to separate oneself entirely from that Church, as well as from the State that established it.

Plymouth Colony was founded by Separatists in 1620. Massachusetts Bay Colony was founded by Puritans in 1630. (There were very few Puritans anywhere in New England between 1620 and 1630.) Plymouth and Massachusetts remained two distinct and independent colonies until 1691, when Plymouth was finally incorporated—much against its will—into Massachusetts. During the decades before 1691 the differences between Separatists and Puritans had been quietly smoothed over, and the two kinds of churches effectively became one denomination, later termed Congregational.

Moreover, between 1620 and 1630 several small settlements had been formed on the territory that would eventually become Massachusetts Bay Colony, for instance at Salem and at Marblehead. These two seaports were founded as commercial ventures, not Separatist refuges or Puritan theocracies. They distanced themselves from the strictest Puritan orthodoxy as much as was prudent and possible.

As already noted, most of Adriana Porter's earliest ancestors settled at Plymouth. Because of this, one can safely say that they were Separatists, not Puritans. Several of them, such as William Brewster, the Teaching Elder of the Church at Plymouth, were clearly committed to that faith. Others, for instance the Billingtons and the Hopkinses, were almost certainly just "going along" with their Separatist neighbors so as to live at peace among them.

Adriana Porter's earliest ancestors at Salem and Marblehead—many of whom were seafarers—would have attended the Puritan Churches there, for those churches were the only ones in town and everyone was obliged by law to attend them. No doubt some of them were convinced Puritans, while others were just obeying the law and "going along" with their neighbors. As already mentioned, a few of them served as ministers in Puritan or Congregational churches.

In view of this ancestry, it might seem odd that Henry Porter, his wife Sarah, his daughter Adriana, his son William, and his son's wife and children were all registered in the 1881 Canadian census not as members of the Congregational Church

18

nor of the established Church of England, but as Baptists. Indeed, nearly all of their Porter, Cook, and Trask relatives at Yarmouth are registered either as Baptists or as Free-will Baptists in that census.[12] However, most of the Protestants in Yarmouth County had become Baptists or Free-will Baptists about two generations earlier, in consequence of a powerful revival movement that swept through Nova Scotia in the years before and just after 1800.[13] Most likely it was Adriana Porter's great-grand-parents who were the first of her ancestors to become Baptists. If so, Adriana and her parents, like most of their closest kin, would simply have been born into families that already considered themselves Baptist.

Baptists, of course, practiced believer's baptism exclusively, and did not have their children baptized as infants. Even adults were not baptized lightly or routinely during the nineteenth century. At that time, a candidate for believer's baptism was expected to have undergone a highly emotional experience of personal conversion, and was usually obliged to provide an account of that experience to the minister for scrutiny—and often also to the entire congregation—before being baptized. Those who had never undergone such an experience were never baptized at any time in their lives, not even on the point of death; neither were they expected or even allowed (in most churches) to share in the other of the two sacraments, that is, to take communion. Paradoxical as it may sound, it was easier and caused less comment to function openly as an unbaptized person in a Baptist church than in a Congregational or Anglican church.

Obviously, on the surface of things the 1881 Canadian census seems to contradict Gwen Thompson's claim that Adriana Porter, Sarah Arnot Cook, and Wealthy Trask were not Christians at all, but Witches. The first two of these women are clearly identified as Baptists there. Moreover, all of Wealthy Trask's children and grandchildren and their families seem to be identified either as Baptists or as Free-will Baptists, which strongly suggests that Wealthy herself would have told the census taker that she was one or the other kind of Baptist had she still been alive in 1881.

Yet a census return can only record what the census taker was told. By itself, it cannot be conclusive evidence of anything—especially not when family secrets are at stake.

Even if these three women were Witches, and not Christians at all, they would hardly have told the census taker so in 1881. Even now, more than a century later, it is not hard to imagine some of the troubles they would have brought upon their own heads if they had identified their religion as Witchcraft. Yet the Canadian census taker was required to ask what each person's religion was, so they could not avoid the official question entirely. The easiest way out would be to name some Christian denomination. Indeed, in those days it would have been very prudent for any Witch to pass as a Christian among her neighbors, to attend some church at least on occasion, and to feign at least a modicum of belief.[14]

If this is what they did, then why did these three women choose to pass as Baptists, rather than as members of some other denomination? There would have been two good reasons for that choice. One was that nearly all of their living relatives, and indeed most of Yarmouth, were Baptists or Free-will Baptists, and conformity is often the safest path. The other was that Baptists are not supposed to baptize their children, and can also avoid being baptized themselves by simply and truthfully stating that they have not (yet) had a true conversion experience.

The United States census takers have never asked any official questions about anyone's religion, and there is no place on United States census schedules to enter any religious information, so one cannot use census returns to learn whether Adriana Porter continued to call herself a Baptist after she emigrated to the United States.

Adriana Porter's Ancestors at Salem in 1692

Adriana Porter was related through each parent to many of the leading men and women of Salem and its nearby towns (such as Beverly), including some of the people most deeply implicated in the witch hunt of 1692. The full history of the Salem witch hunt is easily found elsewhere; here we shall confine our attention to the role played in it by members of the Putnam, Porter, Trask, and Hale families.[15]

Tensions had been running high in Salem and Salem Village (now Danvers) for several years before the witchcraft trials began. The years around 1689-1692 were a time of enormous political uncertainty, when the authority of state and church in New England was shaken to its very foundations and seemed about to topple. King Charles II had revoked the Charter of the Massachusetts Bay Colony in 1684, not long before he died, and transferred all authority to a governor appointed by the King. His successor, James II, appointed governors over New England whose sympathies lay with the Crown and the Church of England. In consequence, the first Anglican Church service was held in Boston in 1686, and soon thereafter a maypole was set up in Charleston—probably the first one in Massachusetts since Thomas Morton's maypole at Merrymount had been cut down in 1628. More seriously, in 1687 the royal governor, Sir Edmund Andros, nullified all private titles to land, which had been the main source of personal and family wealth in New England. Henceforth land in New England could no longer be owned outright by private individuals, but only possessed. Indeed, possession could be maintained only by paying an initial validation fee and a quitrent to the Crown every year. At the same time the royal governor also began to levy taxes by simple decree, without asking for any popular vote to do so.

In 1688, however, James II was driven from the throne of England, to be succeeded by William III and Mary II. In 1689, acting on the authority of the new sovereigns, the leading citizens of Massachusetts deposed and arrested Andros. However, in 1692 a new royal governor was appointed, Sir William Phips. He was a man of great luck but little competence, and during his tenure the royal governor's authority hung by a thread against popular discontent. In effect, there was no real government at all in Massachusetts Bay Colony during those years.

In Salem Village two of the wealthiest men had been John Putnam and John Porter, the founders of the old Salem families that bear those surnames. By 1689 both of these men were long dead, but their extensive lands remained in the hands of their children and grandchildren. Under other circumstances these two wealthy and powerful families might have cooperated, for the arbitrary measures of Sir Edmund Andros threatened each family in the same way and to the same extent. However, other economic factors were also at play. The balance of wealth and power had slowly begun to shift from land to commerce, and this shift strongly favored the Porters, while it strongly disfavored the Putnams. Even before Kings Charles II and James II had plunged the colony into administrative chaos, the Putnams and the Porters were at loggerheads.

Of the second-generation Putnams, the eldest son, Thomas Sr., was the wealthiest, for as eldest son he had inherited a double portion of his father's estate. In turn, his eldest son, Thomas Jr., had long expected to inherit a double share of his father's wealth, which would consolidate his position as head of the extended family in the third generation. (He was in any case the eldest male in the third generation of Putnams, which also enhanced his role as head of the family.) Thomas Jr. had also married well, taking Ann Carr as his wife, whose father had derived great wealth from manufacturing as well as farming; and he expected a fair share of his father-in-law's estate after the old man died.

However, fortune was to deal Thomas Putnam Jr. three heavy blows that wounded his pride and shattered all his high expectations. These blows seem to have goaded him and his immediate family into a deadly fury against the Porters and several other families allied with them. The seeds for two of these three blows had been planted long before, in 1665 and 1666, when his mother died and his father, Thomas Putnam Sr., took a new wife. She was Mary Veren, and she came from a family that had gained its wealth more from trade than from the land. In 1669 she bore Thomas Sr. a son of his old age, whom he named Joseph.

The first of the three blows fell on Thomas Putnam Jr. in 1682, when his father-in-law, George Carr, died, for the widow Carr and her two sons managed effectively to keep his entire estate for themselves, depriving his daughters and their husbands (including Ann Carr and her husband Thomas Putnam Jr.) of any significant part of it.

The second blow fell in 1686, when his own father, Thomas Putnam Sr., died. By his will he left the lion's share of his estate to his second wife and her son Joseph, giving each of the children of his deceased first wife only a relatively small inheritance. He also appointed his wife and her son as executors of his estate and he also chose one of John Porter's sons, Israel, as overseer of his estate. Thus he legally and publicly excluded the children of his first wife from any role in the administration of his estate.

The third and final blow fell in 1690, when his half-brother Joseph chose to marry Elizabeth Porter, one of Israel Porter's daughters.

Eventually a fourth blow fell on Thomas Putnam Jr., but only in 1695. When his stepmother, Mary Veren Putnam, died in that year, she left almost all of her estate to her own son, cutting off Thomas Jr. with a token five shillings because he had "brought upon me inconvenient and unnecessary charges and disbursements at several times"—in fact, he had taken her to court over his father's estate. This will, of course, provoked a new round of challenges in court, all of which Thomas Jr. lost. This seems to have been the last straw. (As mentioned previously, in 1699 Thomas Jr. and his wife died within 15 days of one another, possibly by their own hands.)

The next chapter of the story is well known. When Salem Village came to call a minister in 1689, Thomas Putnam Jr. and his kin favored Samuel Parris, while his half-brother Joseph Putnam and all the Porters set their faces against that appointment. The Putnams prevailed for once, and Samuel Parris took up his duties in a badly divided village. Parris seems to have been a petty, foolish man, obsessed with churchly pomp and his own prosperity and privilege. This only exacerbated the tensions in Salem Village. As things went from bad to worse in his relations with his parish, he saw only the Devil at work and said so again and again in his sermons. In a time of increasing anxiety and extreme social and political instability, his sermons sowed the seeds of disaster.

What brought these seeds to flower was the chance discovery that Samuel Parris's own daughter Elizabeth, together with some of her friends, had been experimenting with the forbidden practices of divination and perhaps also spell casting. This discovery played right into the hands of the minister's opponents in Salem Village. It could easily have put an end to his career as a minister, if scapegoats could not be found. Thomas Putnam Jr. seized the opportunity. He and his family cried "witch" upon all their enemies, claiming that evil witchcraft was the source of all their troubles—the Village's and their own alike.

In the beginning, the Putnams and their kin accused the weak and powerless. Soon, however, they had taken the measure of Samuel Parris, of the judges who presided over the ensuing trials, and of the other ministers who had been called in from other towns for assistance. Among those ministers was John Hale of Beverly, seemingly a man of more learning than common sense. The trials made him a wiser man, but also a sadder one, as can be seen in the insightful book he wrote about them afterwards. The Putnams and their allies refined their methods of accusation, extended their reach, and cautiously began to accuse increasingly powerful rivals and supposed enemies.

Other men in other towns soon saw the usefulness of the witchcraft trials as a way to settle old scores and feather their own nests in the process, and learned from the Putnams' successes. It was not long until the evil spread to Andover and elsewhere.

Soon, however, the accusers overreached themselves and accused the richest and most powerful families of the Colony—according to one source, even the wife of the Royal Governor himself. Not long thereafter Sir William Phips exercised his authority to dissolve the court that was trying the accused, and over the following months he carefully engineered some judicial relief for the accused who were still in prison. He also prevented further executions even of people who had already been sentenced to death for the crime of witchcraft.

By then about 175 people had been imprisoned for witchcraft, and over 200 others accused. (Not one of Adriana Porter's ancestors or even her blood relatives was among them.) Nineteen people had been hanged for that crime, and one pressed to death for refusing to plead to the charge.

Eight more of the accused had died in prison, at least one of them while being kept there after having been found innocent because she could not pay for the costs of her imprisonment. Two or three others were sold into slavery, again to recover the costs of their imprisonment.

Dorcas Good, just four years old, had been kept in prison in chains for nearly nine months, the last six of them by herself after her mother had been executed. As her father wrote in 1710 in a petition for relief, she "was so hardly used and terrified that she has ever since been very chargeable, having little or no reason to govern herself." That is, she had been driven mad by months of isolation and fear.

Eleven of the others accused had been condemned and sentenced to hang, and the death warrants had been signed for eight of them. Though none of the 11 were ever executed, they all lived under attainder for many years. (A person who had been sentenced to death automatically became attainted by virtue of that sentence, but a reprieve did not automatically reverse attainder.) Attainder was a horrible fate, for an attainted person is deprived of all legal standing, rights, and even personhood. In effect, an attainted person counts as an object or a corpse in law, not as a person, even though he or she still lives and may continue to live for decades to come. Two of these eleven attainders were reversed in 1703, eight others in 1711.[16] There seems to be no evidence that the attainder of one of the eleven (Elizabeth Johnson Jr.) was ever reversed.

Most of the people accused of witchcraft at Salem in 1692 were nothing more than victims of their neighbors' wrath and greed. A few of them, however, do appear from the evidence to have made some use of such occult sciences as palmistry or astrology, and a very few seem even to have tried their hand at spell casting.[17] None of them was related by blood to Adriana Porter. Her ancient relatives—the Putnams, the Trasks, the Hales, and the Porters—included the accusers and those who worked behind the scenes to oppose the accusers, but not one of the accused.[18]

Endnotes

1. Brown, George S. Yarmouth, Nova Scotia. *Genealogies, Transcribed from the Yarmouth Herald,* eds. Martha and William Reamy (Baltimore: Genealogical Publishing Co., 1993. [Brøderbund CD #274]), p. 183, 516. (Note that on p. 516 Adriana Porter is mistakenly named Amanda.)

2. One study of the town of Hingham, Massachusetts, during the eighteenth century shows that the names of well over three-fourths of all children who died young were assigned as necronyms to a younger brother or sister. See Daniel Scott Smith, "Child-Naming Practices, Kinship Ties, and Change in Family Attitudes in Hingham, Massachusetts, 1641 to 1880," *Journal of Social History* 18 (1984/5): 541-66. See also David Hackett Fischer, "Forenames and the Family in New England: An Exercise in Historical Onomastics," in *Generations and Change: Genealogical Perspectives in Social History,* eds. Robert M. Taylor and Ralph J. Crandall, Macon, Georgia: Mercer University Press (1986): 215-41.

3. Brown, George S. *Yarmouth, Nova Scotia: A Sequel to Campbell's History.* Boston: Rand Avery, 1888, p. 205. For the history of Yarmouth see also J. R. Campbell. *A History of the County of Yarmouth, Nova Scotia.* St. John, New Brunswick: J. and A. McMillan, 1876; and his *An Answer to Some Strictures in Brown's Sequel to Campbell's History of Yarmouth.* St. John, New Brunswick: J. and A. McMillan, 1889.

4. Brown, George S. Yarmouth, Nova Scotia. *Genealogies, Transcribed from the Yarmouth Herald,* eds. Martha and William Reamy. Baltimore: Genealogical Publishing Co., 1993, [Brøderbund CD #274], p. 183, 516.

5. ibid.

6. According to his death certificate, his parents were Richard Healy and Eliza J. Millitt, both born in Nova Scotia. See Appendix D.

7. According to the *Social Security Death Index* and the *Massachusetts Death Index,* Ola B. Turner Healy Stetson was born May 5, 1903, and died January 10, 1996; Chester D. Stetson was born August 26, 1905 and died July 16, 1993. See Appendix D.

8. Sarah Arnot Cook was a descendant of 23 passengers on the *Mayflower,* namely John Alden; John, Elinor, and Francis Billington; William and Mary Brewster; James, Susanna, and Mary Chilton; Francis Cook; Francis, Sarah, and Samuel Eaton; Samuel Fuller; Stephen and Elizabeth Hopkins; John Howland; William, Alice, and Priscilla Mullins; and John, Joan, and Elizabeth Tilley. This

is not quite half of the 51 passengers who lived long enough to start families of their own in the New World.

9. Robert was pleased to discover that Adriana Porter was a descendant of Mary Chilton in the seventh generation, for he is a descendant of Mary's sister Isabella in the thirteenth generation. He and Adriana are therefore seventh cousins six times removed.

10. Kathleen P. Lamb. *Capt. John Tardy, and Ruth M. Blaney of Marblehead, Mass., to Halifax, Nova Scotia about 1774 and Descendants.* Rockwood, Tenn.: self-published, 1999, p. 1-2.

11. In addition to the genealogical sources cited for Nehemiah Porter Sr. in Appendix A, see Maurice W. Armstrong, *The Great Awakening in Nova Scotia, 1776-1809* Hartford, Conn.: The American Society of Church History (1948): 36, 43, 46, 48.

12. The difference between the two denominations turns on the acceptance of John Calvin's doctrine of Predestination by the Baptists, and the rejection of that doctrine by the Free-will Baptists.

13. Maurice W. Armstrong, *The Great Awakening in Nova Scotia, 1776-1809.* Hartford, Conn.: The American Society of Church History, 1948. According to J. R. Campbell, *A History of the County of Yarmouth, Nova Scotia.* St. John, N. B.: J. and A. McMillan, 1876, 109, the Canadian Census of 1871 revealed that more than half of the inhabitants of Yarmouth County were at that time either Baptists or Free-will Baptists, and not quite a fourth of them were Roman Catholic. Most of the remaining fourth were split among 13 other Protestant denominations. About one-fiftieth of the total claimed to belong to no denomination, and 17 rugged individualists declared that they were "without creed."

14. Indeed, Gerald Gardner firmly insisted that one could be both a Witch and a follower of another religion—even an unorthodox Christian—at the same time. See his *Witchcraft Today.* London: Rider, 1954, p. 121-22; and also J. L. Bracelin. *Gerald Gardner: Witch.* London: Octagon Press, 1960, p. 206.

15. The following four books are enormously valuable, for they give extensive information on the very complex genealogical interrelations between all participants: Paul Boyer and Stephen Nissenbaum, *Salem-Village Witchcraft* (Boston: Northeastern University Press, 1972, rev. ed., 1993), and *Salem Possessed: The Social Origins of Witchcraft* (Cambridge, Mass.: Harvard University Press, 1974); Enders Robinson, *The Devil Discovered: Salem Witchcraft 1692,* 2nd ed. Prospect Heights, Ill.: Waveland Press, 2001; and

Salem Witchcraft and Hawthorne's House of the Seven Gables. Bowie, Md.: Heritage Books, 1992.

16. Enders Robinson. *The Devil Discovered: Salem Witchcraft 1692,* 2nd ed., Prospect Heights, Ill.: Waveland Press, 2001, p. xvi-xvii [only in the 2nd ed.], and his *Salem Witchcraft* and *Hawthorne's House of the Seven Gables.* Bowie, Md.: Heritage Books, 1992, p. 202-04.

17. See the endnotes for Part 3, "Magic and Occult Sciences in Old New England" for references.

18. Gwen Thompson once told one of her early initiates that "the real Witches were sleeping with the witch-hunters" at Salem in 1692 and were not even suspected.

Part 3

What Could Adriana Porter Have Known?

The Persistence of Ancestral Traditions

Old New England families have always taken a very keen interest in their ancestors, and for centuries they have eagerly told and retold ancestral tales. New Englanders began to prepare systematic handwritten accounts of their genealogy as early as the middle of the 1700s, when a few old men and women were still alive who could remember meeting in their youth the last aged survivors of the first voyages to New England in the 1620s and the 1630s. A few of these early genealogical records have come down to us, carefully cherished throughout the intervening centuries. Also toward the end of the eighteenth century genealogies of these families began to appear in print.

New England families did not necessarily lose the taste for ancestral tales when they migrated to Nova Scotia. When Adriana Porter's father and mother were born in 1820 and 1818, respectively, many of the men and women who had first come from New England to Yarmouth in the 1760s and 1770s were still alive and could tell tales of their own ancestors to their children and grandchildren.

Gwen Thompson's surviving letters show that she possessed the New Englander's characteristic interest in her old ancestors. She knew the names and the circumstances of the lives of many of them, and told her initiates stories about some of them. Most of the material in her letters remains oath-bound, naturally enough, so we will have to speculate about possibilities rather than analyze actual examples.

We shall begin by considering a few examples of the steps by which stories about Gwen Thompson's ancestors might have come down from seventeenth-century New England to her grandmother, Adriana Porter, and thence to her. No one knows for certain now whether these particular stories were handed down to her. Our purpose is merely to show how they might have been transmitted across the centuries, so that the reader can understand the process and its attendant difficulties.

Two Trask Examples

We shall take the Salem witch hunt as our first example. In his old age William Trask might well have told stories about the witch hunt, especially if any of his children or grandchildren had asked him why he had moved from Salem to Weymouth around 1700. Suppose that he did tell stories about the events of 1692 and that some of his descendants found them interesting enough to pass them on to their children and grandchildren, and so on through the generations, until these stories reached his great-great-great-granddaughter, Ardiana Porter.

What would be the shortest path that leads through all these generations from William Trask's lips to Adriana Porter's ears? Only four generations separate William Trask from Adriana Porter, so such a story could have been passed down across all those generations with no more than five tellings, from parent to child. The generations are as follows (see the genealogical tables in Appendix A).

- William Trask, 1674 - 1746
- Elias Trask, 1707 - 1780
- John Trask, 1751 - 1833
- Wealthy (Trask) Cook, 1787 - 1832
- Sarah Arnot (Cook) Porter, 1818 - after 1881
- Adriana Porter, 1857 - 1946

However, we should also ask whether this story could be passed down with fewer than five tellings, from grandparent to grandchild or even great-grandchild. If so, what is the least number of tellings needed to span the intervening generations?

The answer can easily be worked out from the dates given above. In this particular example, there is one place where a grandparent could have passed a story directly to a grandchild, for John Trask did not die until his granddaughter, Sarah Arnot Cook, was about 15 years old. The *shortest possible "vertical" chain of transmission,* that is, in the direct line of descent, from William Trask to Adriana Porter, needs only four tellings.

Can we shorten the chain of transmission further by allowing for other possibilities within the family? In this particular case we can. Wealthy (Trask) Cook had an older sister, Elizabeth (Trask) Tinkham, who died in 1863, when Adriana Porter was six years old. If we allow for the possibility of a "diagonal" transmission from this elderly great-aunt to her very young great-niece, then we can shorten the chain of transmission to just three tellings.

In this fashion one can always work out the *shortest possible chain of transmission* for any particular story, whether vertical (i.e., in a direct line of descent) or diagonal (i.e., by any other route through the family tree).

We could apply the same methods to a different Trask family story, this time a tale about how William Trask's immigrant ancestor (his grandfather, also named William Trask) had left East Coker, Somerset County, England, in 1624 and crossed the Atlantic to New England. If we did so, we would have to add two more tellings to the chain of transmission, for the first William Trask died in 1666, eight years before his grandson William was born. (In this particular case, there seems to be no easy way to shorten the chain by taking diagonal chains of transmission into account.)

In fact, Gwen Thompson did know that her Trask ancestor came from Somerset Co., England, in the early 1600s. At least that one small detail may have been correctly passed down to her through no fewer than six tellings.[1]

A Brewster Example

Adriana Porter was a great-great-great-great-great-great-granddaughter of Jonathan Brewster, who was the eldest living son of William Brewster, the first Teaching Elder of Plymouth Church. Jonathan had studied at the University of Leyden before coming to Plymouth in 1621 on the *Fortune.* Toward the end of his life, he carried out alchemical experiments in a laboratory at his trading post on Brewster's Neck (now in the town of New London, Connecticut). A few of his alchemical letters have survived, which display great self-assurance. He wrote them in 1656 to his fellow alchemist, John Winthrop Jr. (who was also the governor of the Colony of Connecticut). In these letters Jonathan claimed that he had finally learned how to make the Red Elixir and the White Elixir, and that he hoped to have discovered the ultimate secrets of the Alchemical Art within a very few years. Meanwhile he was keeping his work secret from everyone. Not even his wife and children knew what he was doing in his private laboratory.[2]

In 1659, however, Jonathan Brewster died without making a will. When his estate was settled, all his possessions had to be carefully examined and valued by his executors, and other people would have entered his secret laboratory at last. Along with the rest of his family, his grown daughter Mary might have heard something of her father's alchemy at that time. If it had caught her interest, she might have told her children about it, and so on. In this way it might have come down across the six generations that separated her from Adriana Porter. These generations are the following:

- Mary (Brewster) Turner, 1627 - ca. 1698
- Ruth (Turner) Prince, 1663 - 1729
- Ruth (Silvester) Cook, 1701 - about 1779
- George Ring, 1726 - 1776
- Louisa (Ring) Cook, 1748 - 1826
- John Cook, 1776 - 1875
- Sarah Arnot (Cook) Porter, 1818 - after 1881
- Adriana Porter, 1857 - 1946

In this example, too, one should ask, what is the shortest possible *vertical chain of transmission* that can be constructed between Mary Brewster and Adriana Porter? It requires just five tellings to span the 200 years between Jonathan Brewster's death and Adriana Porter's birth, if one allows for transmission from grandmother to granddaughter in the two places where that could have happened. Here is this shortest possible vertical chain of transmission:

- Mary (Brewster) Turner, 1627 - ca. 1698
- Ruth (Turner) Prince, 1663 - 1729
- Ruth (Silvester) Cook, 1701 - about 1779
- Louisa (Cook) Ring, 1748 - 1826
- Sarah Arnot (Cook) Porter, 1818 - after 1881
- Adriana Porter, 1857 - 1946

All this is hypothetical, of course, no amount of *mights* can ever add up to one *did.* The point of this example is not to ask whether Adriana Porter actually heard a family story about her ancestor's work in alchemy, but only to show that such a story could have been handed down across 200 years with no more than five tellings.

The Evaluation of these Possibilities

So we see that family stories and ancestral tales could be handed down over a rather long span of years with surprisingly few tellings and retellings. Of course this may seem unlikely to modern Americans, when family storytelling has been reduced almost to a lost art by the relentless pressure of mass media of information and entertainment. Yet the art and practice of family storytelling is not wholly extinct even now, and countless earlier works of literature by New England authors depict it in full bloom.

It is instructive to read a few passages from John Greenleaf Whittier's famous poem *Snowbound* (1865), which brings to life the role that storytelling held within his family circle when he was a boy. He describes an evening around the hearth after a great snowstorm in December had cut neighbor off from neighbor and brought all outdoor work to a halt.

> Shut in from all the world without,
> We sat the clean-winged hearth about,
> Content to let the north-wind roar
> In baffled rage at pane and door,
> While the red logs before us beat
> The frost-line back with tropic heat;
> .....
>
> And, for the winter fireside meet,
> Between the andirons' straddling feet,
> The mug of cider simmered slow,
> The apples sputtered in a row,
> And, close at hand, the basket stood
> With nuts from brown October's wood
> .....
>
> We sped the time with stories old,
> Wrought puzzles out, and riddles told,
> .....
>
> Our father rode again his ride
> On Memphremagog's wooded side;
> Sat down again to moose and samp
> In trapper's hut and Indian camp;
> .....
>
> Our mother, while she turned her wheel
> Or run the new-knit stocking-heel,
> Told how the Indian hordes came down
> At midnight on Cocheco town,
> And how her own great-uncle bore
> His cruel scalp-mark to fourscore.
> Recalling, in her fitting phrase,
> .....

The story of her early days, -
She made us welcome to her home;
Old hearths grew wide to give us room;
We stole with her a frightened look
At the gray wizard's conjuring-book,
The fame whereof went far and wide
Through all the simple countryside;
.....

Our uncle, innocent of books,
Was rich in lore of fields and brooks,
The ancient teachers never dumb
Of Nature's unhoused lyceum.
In moons and tides and weather wise,
He read the clouds as prophecies,
And foul or fair could well divine,
By many an occult hint and sign,
Holding the cunning-warded keys
To all the woodcraft mysteries;
Himself to nature's heart so near
That all her voices in his ear
Of beast or bird had meanings clear,
Like Apollonius of old,
Who knew the tales the sparrows told,
Or Hermes, who interpreted
What the sage cranes of Nilus said;
.....

Brisk wielder of the birch and rule,
The master of the district school
Held at the fire his favored place;
.....

Happy the snow-locked homes wherein
He tuned his merry violin,
.....

Or mirth-provoking versions told
Of classic legends rare and old,
Wherein the scenes of Greece and Rome
Had all the commonplace of home,
And little seemed at best the odds
'Twixt Yankee peddlers and old gods;
.....

34

The reader, we trust, will immediately have been struck by the mention of "the gray wizard's conjuring-book," which the poet's mother had seen as a girl. What sort of man might her "gray wizard" have been, and how did he and his book end up in rural New Hampshire in the late 1700s? In his foreword to the poem, Whittier explains that the book was once the property of "Bantam the sorcerer," one of the "strange people who lived on the Pisquataqua and Cocheco," and he identifies it as a copy of the 1651 edition of the English translation of Henry Cornelius Agrippa's *Three Books of Occult Philosophy.* Whittier tells a little more about this man in his earlier work, *The Supernaturalism of New England* (1847). He was a Quaker, a "quiet, meek-spirited old man," who was regarded as "a conjurer, and skillful adept in the art of magic"; and he did the customary work of a village cunning-man for his neighbors "without money and without price." The book itself, Whittier wrote in 1847, "is still in possession of the conjurers family." As we shall see in the next chapter, such people were not particularly rare in old New England.

Otherwise Whittier mentions tales of far travels, of war, of even older customs and ways of life fading into memory by the early 1800s, of hunting and fishing and all the lore of nature, of local legends and of the myths of ancient Greece and Rome—of "Yankee peddlers and old gods." This was New England, and these were its stories told at the hearth, not all that many years after Adriana Porter's ancestors left its shores for Nova Scotia.

In such an environment Ardiana Porter is quite likely to have heard many tales of her ancestors and their doings even as far back as two centuries before her grandparents' birth—and that is all the time that separated her grandparents from young William Trask growing up in Somerset County, not yet resolved to sail for New England.

However, time has its way with every tale handed down by word of mouth from the past. The content and emphasis change a little with every retelling, and each storyteller freely invents the details that she does not happen to know, but must supply if her story is to hold her audience. A tale told about a Trask ancestor who left Salem in disgust after the Salem witch hunt can easily be transmuted into a tale about an ancestor who was unjustly accused of witchcraft at Salem and had to leave. A few more retellings, and that same ancestor may well seem to be an actual Witch, who barely escaped from Salem with his life.

And so it goes. It does not stretch the probabilities very far to suppose that Adriana Porter, who was born in 1856, could have had many stories to tell about her ancestors, or that in her old age she could have told them to her young granddaughter to pass the hours. Like nearly all such stories, her stories would likely have contained bits of truth under all the distortions that naturally arise from telling and retelling. Yet no story is likely to be wholly true after many retellings, when several centuries separate the storyteller from the events themselves. The question is always, how to separate the grains of wheat from all the chaff.

Magic and the Occult Sciences in Old New England

Let us return now to Bantam, the "gray wizard" mentioned in Whittier's poem, a Quaker who also did the work of a traditional English cunning-man. Whittier tells us that he lived in Somersworth, New Hampshire. He was a real person, named Ambrose Bantam, who can be found listed in the 1790 United States census as the head of a small family.

Was Bantam an unparalleled rarity in old New England, or were such people more common than we now realize? As it turns out, they were not rare, though scholars have only quite recently discovered the fact. It was always just a question of looking in the right places to find them.

Cunning-men and cunning-women, fortune-tellers, palmists, glass-lookers (scryers), rods-men (dowsers), vendors of charms and other small magics—even an occasional conjurer of spirits, astrologer, or alchemist—will not usually be found among the urban elite of New England. Instead, they lived and worked in the isolated rural communities, and they usually kept a low profile. They also plied their trades in seaports, for sailors have always eagerly bought charms and spells against the great hazards of their work.

George Lyman Kittredge long ago recognized that there was a great continuity in these practices between England and New England, as was only to be expected.[3] This was merely the natural consequence of the fact that there were a great many cunning-folk and other such people in old England at the time, and by chance alone some of them would have been part of the vast emigration to New England that occurred in the 1600s.[4] But it is only within the last 15 years or so that much work has been done to trace the lives of these people in the extant records. Richard Godbeer has examined much of the evidence for seventeenth-century New England. The various occult and magical practices that he found to be widespread in New England were, as expected, the practices that were also current in England during the same century.[5]

A list compiled by Peter Benes identified 90 such people who had flourished in New England between 1644 and 1850; and Benes suspected that he had only scratched the surface. As we already mentioned, a few of the men and women accused of the crime of witchcraft in 1692 at Salem and elsewhere fall into this category—even though none of them may have been witches as defined in the laws of the time or Witches in the modern sense of the word—and their names are on Benes's list.[6]

Godbeer's work was preceded by that of D. Michael Quinn, who took a close look at the historical background of early Mormonism and the family of its founder, Joseph Smith Jr., and followed up old hints that the Smith family had been very deeply involved with a subculture of magic that had flourished in New England and upstate New York during the 1700s and the early 1800s.[7] A few years later, John L. Brooke followed the same hints about the Smiths in a somewhat different direction and found the persistence of occult and hermetic teachings as well as alchemy and ceremonial magic throughout the same regions during the same centuries.[8]

The many specific pieces of evidence that these two historians of early Mormonism found were far more numerous and varied than anyone had ever suspected. They found, for example, general stores that advertised lists of current and antiquarian books on the occult sciences for sale, and traveling spirit-conjurers who also dabbled in alchemy and counterfeiting when the opportunity presented itself.

Quinn even published a photograph of a curiously engraved, hand-forged, black-handled, double-edged knife that had come down in the family of Joseph Smith Jr.'s brother, Hiram, and was originally made for their father, Joseph Smith Sr. As Quinn realized, the engravings on the blade of this knife, as well as various sigils on several other artifacts that had once been owned by these three Smiths, had been copied from H. C. Agrippa's *Three Books of Occult Philosophy* (published in 1651 in English translation) and from Reginald Scot's *The Discovery of Witchcraft* (published in 1584, 1651 and 1665), or perhaps from some later book that drew on Agrippa and Scot.[9]

Nor have these scholars exhausted the available evidence. One can also document, for instance, a manuscript copy (said to have been made in 1512) of the grimoire called *Lemegeton* that had once been owned by a high-ranking military officer, Ethan Allen Hitchcock, who was one of Edgar Allen Poe's instructors at West Point, and who later wrote extensively on alchemy.[10]

In short, evidence can probably be found for the existence of any occult or magical practice whatsoever in old New England, provided only that it can also be found in England as well. The myth of a Puritan New England, where occultism and magic were rare, and quickly stamped out whenever they appeared, is no more than a myth. The reality was very different indeed.

Bluenose Folklore at Yarmouth

We have seen that Adriana Porter spent the first thirty-odd years of her long life living with her parents at Yarmouth, before she moved to New England sometime between 1881 and 1887. What could she have learned about occultism and esotericism, about magic and witchcraft, while growing up in Yarmouth?

When Adriana Porter was still a child, the town of Yarmouth was a prosperous seaport, drawing its wealth from trade, fishing, and shipbuilding. Like every Atlantic seaport, it had always been home to a number of women (and occasionally men) who made and sold charms and amulets to sailors and fishermen; who told the best and worst times to set out to sea; who claimed the skill to alleviate illness or bring it on, and to find lost or stolen property; who might give a young woman the sight of her future husband; who would dare to lay a ghost or banish an evil spirit—who, it was rumored, might even cast a spell now and then. Even though such people kept a very low profile, we can still name several dozen of them who plied their trade in New England seaports such as York, Newburyport, Gloucester, Marblehead, Salem, Tiverton, Newport, and Providence during the 1700s and 1800s; the number of those who left no trace must be substantially higher. Like any other young person in humble circumstances, even in the 1860s and 1870s, Adriana Porter could have found several such people in Yarmouth, had she wished to.

Even if she had never felt a need for the services of such experts, Adriana Porter grew up in a world that was still rich in all sorts of traditional lore: times to plant each vegetable and fruit and times to harvest it, the many signs of fair weather and foul, the vital lore of pregnancy and birthing, omens of sickness and death. In that world lived men and women who claimed the ability to see presages of death ("forerunners," as such sights were called), and whole families who were said to be gifted with "foresight" or—less commonly—with "hindsight," that is, the troublesome ability to look into the future or the distant past. Much of this lore was captured in proverbs and rhymes that were often repeated by the old and unconsciously learned by the young. These were just as essential a part of a young woman's upbringing as learning to sew a neat seam, to make a pudding, to trim a lamp, or to bank a fire—tasks that must be done just so or else. All of Nova Scotia was particularly rich in lore of this sort, as well as English traditional songs and stories about ghosts and witches. Here are some examples, collected by Helen Creighton during the years between 1928 and 1968.[11]

¤ A woman told of a witch trying to teach her to be a witch. She used to come here from Dover and stay. The witch liked her and asked her if she'd like to learn to bewitch people and have fun. She got to telling her what she'd have to do. She had to sign a

38

lease of her life to the devil, curse her father and mother, cut her finger and sign her name in the blood. That was enough and she wouldn't go any further. She was 16 at the time and had thought it would be fun to go through a keyhole.

¤ Mother told me the witch takes a candle and sticks pins in it (this was at Ostrea Lake). Whoever put the spell on the animal will come to the house and ask for something (borrow). One came at 12 o'clock at night and they knew she had put the spell on the cow.

¤ It used to be a custom to build a coin right into the door leading to the animals to keep evil spirits off.

¤ Money was put under the masts of ships when being built to bring prosperity.

¤ Always turn a ship with the sun. It is bad luck to turn her against the sun, even if it takes a long time to do it the other way.

¤ On Hallowe'en Night take the skull bone of a man and put it down. Fire at the moon and three drops of blood will come from the moon and fall in the eye of this skull bone. Take it and run a ball into the eye of that person and put it in a gun and you can fire at any enemy at all. If that ball won't find the enemy and kill him, the ball would come back and go in your own pocket.

¤ On Hallowe'en night go down the cellar steps backwards and look in a mirror and you will see the face of your future husband.

¤ Green Christmas, full graveyard.

¤ Look over your left shoulder when you see the new moon and make a wish.

¤ If you see the new moon through glass, go outside and face the moon and bow three times to it.

¤ A baby born with a caul over its head will never be drowned.

¤ A child born with a caul has second sight; my brother had one and he saw a drowning before it happened, and other things.

¤ Three lights in a room upset a ship at sea.

¤ A woman couldn't tell another woman how to charm. It must be a man.

¤   Carry a blue potato for rheumatism.

¤   Anything that grows under the ground, plant in the dead of the moon; anything above ground, in the growing moon. Any time after the full moon is the dead of the moon.

There are many echoes of this kind of traditional lore as we shall show in detail.

Magic, Occultism, and Alternative Religion in Boston and its Vicinity

Sometime between 1881 and 1887 Adriana Porter left Nova Scotia for New England, where she greatly improved her circumstances by marrying a man whose fortune was rising. She spent most of the rest of her life in Boston and in Melrose, which is only a few miles north of Boston. No longer did she live in a traditional, somewhat decaying Yankee seaport, but in and near one of the wealthiest and most sophisticated cities on the East Coast, up to the minute with each new trend and development.

It must be emphasized that Adriana Porter Healy would have had more leisure time than many women of her age, since her husband was well able to support his family by his own efforts and they had only one child. Of course, like any new mother, she would have been very busy raising her child for the first five or 10 years after his birth in 1895; and she always had to keep house for her family. During most of the last 40 years of her life, however, she would have had a certain amount of free time and money, certainly enough to pursue her own interests, whatever they may have been.

If Adriana Porter had wished to occupy herself with occultism and esotericism, with alternative religions, or even with magic and witchcraft, what would she have been able to find in and near Boston between about 1900 and 1946?

The decades after about 1875 were a time when alternative religions, spiritualities, and ritual organizations flourished in the United States as never before, and Boston was a center of each and every one of them. Listed are several of the most significant of these movements and organizations that were found in Boston and Eastern Massachusetts during the first half of the twentieth century.

- Freemasonry
- The Church of the New Jerusalem (Swedenborgianism)
- Spiritualism
  » Reincarnationalist Spiritualism

- » Anti-reincarnationalist Spiritualism
- Rosicrucianism
  - » Rosicrucian Society in America (Societas Rosicruciana in America)
  - » Brotherhood of the Rose Cross (Fraternitas Rosae Crucis)
  - » Ancient and Mystical Order of the Rose Cross (A.M.O.R.C.)
  - » Rosicrucian Fellowship
- The Metaphysical Movement
  - » Christian Science
  - » Divine Science
  - » New Thought
- Occultism
  - » The Theosophical Society
  - » The Order of the Temple of the Orient (O.T.O.)

There was considerable overlap in membership between many of these movements and organizations. More often than not, a committed member of one of them would at least explore others from time to time, and there were also many people who moved from one organization to another and then another without making a strong commitment to any one of them. For our purposes, the most significant of these movements are Spiritualism, Rosicrucianism, the Theosophical Society, and New Thought.

Spiritualism, with its seances and spirit circles, appeared around 1848 and overran the land like wildfire. By the year 1870 an estimated 7,000,000 Americans either counted themselves as committed Spiritualists, or least attended seances from time to time and favored Spiritualist doctrines. By 1870, Spiritualism had split into several factions, one of which may truly be characterized as the magical wing of Spiritualism. Its best-known advocates were Paschal Beverly Randolph and Emma Hardinge Britten. During her first years in the United States, Helena Petrovna Blavatsky was also reckoned among the magical Spiritualists. Although Spiritualism denied the possibility of reincarnation at first, a major schism eventually arose within the movement over just that question.

Paschal Beverly Randolph (1825-1875) was not only a Spiritualist, but also a magician and a Rosicrucian, and the founder of the first Rosicrucian organizations in English-speaking North America. (There probably were earlier Rosicrucians among the German-speaking immigrants to Pennsylvania.) Randolph had many followers in Boston. He died in 1875, but his teachings were taken up by others, and today are carried on by the Brotherhood of the Rose Cross (with headquarters in

Pennsylvania). The Rosicrucian Society in America was formed in Boston, but it can trace its ancestry back to the well-known Societas Rosicruciana in Anglia (S.R.I.A.), from which also came the occultists who founded the Hermetic Order of the Golden Dawn in London in 1888. The other two Rosicrucian groups listed above had their headquarters in California (the Rosicrucian Fellowship in Oceanside, the A.M.O.R.C. in San Jose), and are less important for our purposes. Each of these four organizations offered its own course of occult training and study, and each appears to have had its own ritual practices.[12]

Emma Hardinge Britten (1823-1899) was born in England, where she spent her youth and her old age, but during her most active years in the middle of her life she lived in the United States, generally in Boston and New York. She was a medium, a trance-speaker, and a pillar of early Spiritualism, as well as the first significant historian of Spiritualism. Before Emma was 13 years old, she had begun to support herself by working as a seer, a crystal gazer, and a "flying soul" (that is, doing astral projection) for a mysterious occult society in England. In her late twenties and early thirties she developed as a spirit medium and trance speaker, and then as a Spiritualist teacher. In her numerous articles she sometimes emphasized that she was not a Christian, and once in a while she referred to herself as a Witch. She believed that magicians, witches, prophets, and spirit mediums were all using the same set of occult powers whether they worked magic and witchcraft, prophesied, or talked with the dead and with spirits who had never been human.[13]

In 1876 Emma Hardinge Britten edited and published two extraordinary books about magic, which she ascribed to an anonymous European adept, Chevalier Louis de B—, who had been a member of the occult society for which Emma had worked 40 years earlier as a child seer. One of these works, *Ghost Land: or, Researches into the Mysteries of Occultism: Illustrated in a Series of Autobiographical Sketches* (Boston, 1867) is a romantic account of Chevalier Louis's life and adventures as an occultist and adept. The other work, which was titled *Art Magic; or, Mundane, Sub-Mundane and Super-Mundane Spiritism: A Treatise . . . Descriptive of Art Magic, Spiritism, the Different Orders of Spirits in the Universe Known to Be Related to, or in Communion with Man* (Boston, 1876), was far more significant. *Art Magic* gave a provocative and thoughtful synthesis of the doctrines and practices of Renaissance Ceremonial Magic and Witchcraft with those of Spiritualism and Mesmerism. It soon became an underground classic, rarely cited but highly influential.[14] Both works were reprinted several times at low cost between 1897 and 1909, and thus were widely available when Adriana Porter had the time and money to pursue her own interests at length.

In the early 1870s Helena Petrovna Blavatsky (1831-1891) crossed the Atlantic to New York and suddenly made a grand entrance on the Spiritualist scene with her claims of extraordinary powers as a medium and an occultist, which she claimed were much the same thing. She very soon caught the notice of Emma Hardinge Britten, and the two worked together for a short while, together with several less-talented men whose interest they had attracted to the enterprise, to found the Theosophical Society. The two women soon parted ways, and Blavatsky left for India, taking most of what was left of the Theosophical Society with her. Yet this was just a temporary setback, for in India she revived the moribund Society, and with the aid of her protégés, Henry Steele Olcott and William Quan Judge, she set it on the road to influence and prestige among occultists of all kinds. The Theosophical Society soon became an organization where occultists of all kinds might meet in almost any part of the world to discuss their shared interests. It inspired many people who might otherwise never have followed up a modest interest in esoteric subjects, and its journals and regional libraries were a resource for such people in their further studies.[15]

Among the many people inspired by the Theosophical Society was a one-time Spiritualist medium, stage magician and performer, and very shrewd business-woman, Anna Eva Fay, who settled in Melrose later in her life. Presumably she was also a Theosophist, for in 1908 she attempted to found a College of Theosophy in Melrose Highlands.[16] This fact testifies to an interest in Theosophy in that part of Massachusetts. William and Adriana (Porter) Healy moved to Melrose in 1906. It would be interesting to know whether this was merely a coincidence, or whether Adriana took any particular interest in Anna Eva Fay's venture. Perhaps further research in the Melrose newspapers will shed some light on the question.

The last of the movements to be mentioned here is New Thought, which is a part of the so-called Metaphysical Movement.[17] This new religious movement was launched by the heroic efforts of Mary Baker Eddy (1821-1910), whose remarkable work, *Science and Health,* was published in 1875 in Boston, and has remained continuously in print from that year up to now. At the heart of Eddy's teaching lay the notion that all matter was ultimately the creation of human thought, and what human thought had made, it could unmake, if only it could gain the necessary skill and power. In short, matter was wholly subject to mind: the slogan "mind over matter" neatly summarizes her insight. She promptly began to develop her own skill and power, and set out to teach others to do the same.

Eddy originally developed her doctrine and practice as a means of healing, and she believed that before her discovery, Jesus was the only person who had ever taught the same doctrine and used the same practice as she did. But "mind over matter" is not at all far removed from magic, and soon some of the people whom she had taught or who had studied her book saw the possibilities for both good and evil. The rest of Eddy's long life was a vain struggle to retain some sort of ownership over her discovery and to contain the harm that she was sure would follow if others could use "mind over matter" however they liked. It was an impossible task, and she failed at it. Others built on it, developed it in many directions, and wrote countless books about it.

Out of this chaos there eventually emerged a single organization, The First Church of Christ, Scientist, that followed Eddy's wishes to the letter, and exerted great control over all other Christian Science Churches anywhere in the world, as well as a number of other churches, schools, and teachers that had built on the foundation she had laid, but not at all according to the plans she had drawn up. These other churches, schools, and teachers are all collectively termed the New Thought movement.

Like Spiritualism, New Thought also developed an openly magical wing, which found its foremost spokesman in the person of William Walker Atkinson (1862-1932). He was a very prolific writer, the author of about 60 books under his own name, 14 more under the name of Yogi Ramacharaka, 10 more as Theron Q. Dumont, and probably one more as Theodore Sheldon. He was the first of the "Three Initiates"—if not all three Initiates rolled into one man—who wrote the esoteric work called *The Kybalion* (1908), and he probably wrote most or all of the curriculum for the "Arcane Teaching" that was circulated from one of his publishing houses. Many of Atkinson's books are manuals of "mind-over-matter" magic, notably two works published in 1907 under the titles, *The Secret of Mental Magic: A Course of Seven Lessons* and *Mental Fascination.*[18] The two works were soon combined into a single volume, which first appeared in 1908 as *Mind-Power; or, The Law of Dynamic Mentation* and then in 1912 as *Mind-Power: The Secret of Mental Magic.* Like Eddy's *Science and Health,* Atkinson's *Mind-Power* has remained continuously in print ever since its first publication.

All these spirits, elementals, seances, scrying, trance-work, astral projection, mind-over-matter practices, esotericism, occultism, magic (and witchcraft), cryptic societies of Freemasons, Rosicrucians, and Theosophists, and a whole host of lesser things combined to make a very heady brew during the first half of the twentieth century. The chief place in all New England where one could drink one's fill of this brew was undoubtedly the city of Boston and the towns nearby—just the places where Adriana Porter lived from about 1900 until her death in 1946. It is impossible to say, from the evidence available so far, whether she actually did drink from this brew, and if so, just how deeply she drank from it. But she undoubtedly had both the free time and the money to do so if she wished. There can be no doubt as to the possibility.

Endnotes

1. Only around 1900 did genealogists independently document that William Trask had been born and raised in Somerset County. This fact was then mentioned in a few books and articles. One must allow for the possibility that Gwen learned it from some close relative who had a strong interest in genealogy and found the information in print.

2. *Collections of the Massachusetts Historical Society,* 4th series, 7 (1865) [= *The Winthrop Papers,* part II], p. 66-87, also plate II (a facsimile of Jonathan Brewster's seal, depicting the all-seeing eye).

3. George Lyman Kittredge. *Witchcraft in Old and New England.* Cambridge, Mass.: Harvard University Press, 1928.

4. For cunning-men in England, see the summary of previous research by Ronald Hutton, *The Triumph of the Moon: A History of Modern Pagan Witchcraft.* Oxford: Oxford University Press, 1999, chapter 6; and now especially Owen Davies, *A People Bewitched: Witchcraft and Magic in Nineteenth-Century Somerset.* Bruton, Somerset: Bruton Press, 1999; *Witchcraft, Magic, and Culture, 1736-1951.* Manchester: Manchester University Press, 1999; and *Cunning-Folk: Popular Magic in English History.* London: Hambledon & London, 2003.

5. Richard Godbeer, *The Devil's Dominion: Magic and Religion in Early New England.* Cambridge: Cambridge University Press, 1992. See also his article, "Chaste and Unchaste Covenants: Witchcraft and Sex in Early Modern Culture," *Wonders of the Invisible World: 1600-1900.* The Dublin Seminar for New England Folklife, Annual Proceedings [vol. 17] (1992): 53-72.

6. Peter Benes, "Fortunetellers, Wise-Men, and Magical Healers in New England, 1644-1850," *Wonders of the Invisible World: 1600-1900.* The Dublin Seminar for New England Folklife, Annual Proceedings [vol. 17] (1992): 127-48.

7. D. Michael Quinn, *Early Mormonism and the Magical World View,* rev. ed. Salt Lake City: Signature Books, 1998.

8. John L. Brooke, *The Refiner's Fire: The Making of Mormon Cosmology, 1644-1844* (Cambridge: Cambridge University Press, 1994. See also his article, " 'The True Spiritual Seed': Sectarian Religion and the Persistence of the Occult in Eighteenth-Century New England," *Wonders of the Invisible World: 1600-1900.* The Dublin Seminar for New England Folklife, Annual Proceedings [vol. 17] (1992): 107-26. See further Laurence A. Johnson, "The 'Money Diggers' of Rose," *New York Folklore Quarterly* 13 (1957): 215-17; Alan

Taylor, "The Early Republic's Supernatural Economy: Treasure Seeking in the American Northeast, 1780-1830," *American Quarterly* 38 (1986): 6-34; and W. R. Jones, " 'Hill-Diggers' and 'Hell-Raisers': Treasure Hunting and the Supernatural in Old and New England," *Wonders of the Invisible World: 1600-1900,* The Dublin Seminar for New England Folklife, Annual Proceedings [vol. 17] (1992): 97-106.

9. D. Michael Quinn. *Early Mormonism and the Magical World View,* rev ed. Salt Lake City: Signature Books, 1998, chapters 3-4, figures 27-82.

10. I. Bernard Cohen. "Ethan Allen Hitchcock: Soldier – Humanitarian – Scholar – Discoverer of the 'True Subject' of the Hermetic Art," *Proceedings of the American Antiquarian Society* 61 (1951): 29-136. Cohen includes a facsimile reprint of the 1862 catalogue of Hitchcock's "books on hermetic philosophy" which were being offered as a single lot for sale at auction; Hitchcock's *Lemegeton* manuscript is the last item in the catalogue, no. 318.

11. Helen Creighton. *Bluenose Magic: Popular Beliefs and Superstitions in Nova Scotia.* Toronto: The Ryerson Press, 1968, p. 19, 21, 50, 119-20, 131-32, 140, 145, 149, 205, 226, 271.

12. John Patrick Deveney. *Paschal Beverly Randolph: A Nineteenth-Century Black American Spiritualist, Rosicrucian and Sex Magician.* Albany: State University of New York Press, 1997; Christopher McIntosh. *The Rosicrucians: The History, Mythology, and Rituals of an Esoteric Order,* 3rd ed. York Beach, Me.: Samuel Weiser, 1997, chapter 12.

13. Robert Mathiesen. "The Unseen Worlds of Emma Hardinge Britten: Some Chapters in the History of Western Occultism," *Theosophical History Occasional Papers,* vol. IX. Fullerton, Calif.: Theosophical History, 2001.

14. It is worth noting that one of Gerald Gardner's earliest initiates, Doreen Valiente, was well acquainted with *Art Magic,* which she cited in her first major work, *An ABC of Witchcraft, Past and Present.* London: Robert Hale, 1973, p. 116.

15. Michael Gomes. *The Dawning of the Theosophical Movement.* Wheaton, Ill.: Theosophical Publishing House, 1987; and Joscelyn Godwin. *The Theosophical Enlightenment.* Albany: State University of New York Press, 1994, are particlarly relevant here.

16. Barry H. Wiley, "The Fay Family Fight," *The Yankee Magic Collector* 1(1983), more accessible online at <www.uelectric.com/pastimes/fay.htm>; Massimo Polidoro, "Anna Eva Fay: The Mentalist Who Baffled Sir William Crookes," *Skeptical Inquirer* 24/1 (January-February 2000): 36-9.

17. Charles S. Braden. *Spirits in Rebellion: The Rise and Development of New Thought.* Dallas: Southern Methodist University Press, 1963; J. Stillson Judah, *The History and Philosophy of the Metaphysical Movements in America.* Philadelphia: The Westminster Press, 1967; Beryl Satter. *Each Mind a Kingdom: American Women, Sexual Purity, and the New Thought Movement, 1875-1920.* Berkeley, Los Angeles, London: University of California Press, 1999.

18. The remnants of Gerald Gardner's library now in Toronto include a copy of Atkinson's *The Secret of Mental Magic.* Echoes of its language can be found in the text "To Help the Sick" in Gardner's manuscript *Ye Bok of ye Art Magical,* which was published by Aidan A. Kelly, *Crafting the Art of Magic, Book I: A History of Modern Witchcraft, 1939-1964.* St. Paul, Minn.: Llewellyn, 1991, p. 77-80.

OLA HEALY - 1922
MOTHER OF LADY GWEN

GWEN'S MOTHER OLA,
GRANDMOTHER ADRIANNA AND
LADY GWEN - MID 1940s

WALTER ELLSWORTH HEALY
DIED 1931 - FATHER OF LADY GWEN

PHYLLIS RUTH HEALY
AGE 16 MONTHS

LADY GWEN AT THE COVENSTEAD OF
LADY KERRY AND STOCK - 1974

LADY GWEN NOVEMBER 1977
SHREVEPORT, LOUISIANA

LADY GWEN - DEVIL'S HOP YARD
CONNECTICUT

LADY GWEN BURIED WITH HER FATHER
WALTER ELLSWORTH HEALY BESIDE HER
PATERNAL GRANDPARENTS.

Part 4

A Close Look at *The Rede of the Wiccae*

The Text

Gwen Thompson published just one brief text from her *Book*. It appeared in print in 1975 under the title "The Rede of the Wiccae" as a part of her article *Wiccan-Pagan Potpourri* on pages 9-11 of the Ostara 1975 issue of *Green Egg*. For easy reference, the *Rede* (as we shall call it) is reprinted on the following pages exactly as it appeared in that article. (The entire article can be found reprinted in Appendix E.)

As we already noted, Gwen Thompson's own *Book* had the form of loose pages in a three-ring binder. The texts on these pages (as Gwen told her initiates) were her copies of the bundle of loose papers tied up in a faded red ribbon that she had inherited from her grandmother in 1946. She destroyed these papers after she had copied them. However, most of the pages now in Gwen's own *Book* are not her earliest copies of these texts. As her initiates can confirm, Gwen often recopied individual pages in her *Book* as they aged and faded, or because thought she could make them look nicer—or simply because she felt like doing so. She continued to recopy individual pages up to the end of her life in 1986. Whenever she recopied a page, she destroyed her earlier copy. We must allow for the possibility that she recopied the pages with the *Rede* more than once, and that the pages with the *Rede* now in her own *Book* were copied around 1975, or even after that year.

Some light can be shed on this by carefully comparing the printed text of the *Rede* with the handwritten text now in Gwen's own *Book,* and also with copies made from Gwen's *Book* by her earliest initiates in the years before 1975. (Two such earlier copies are available to Theitic, which were made in the years 1972 and 1973.)

The handwritten text of the *Rede* now in Gwen Thompson's own *Book* is found on both sides of a single sheet of paper. There is no other text on these two pages, only the *Rede.* As it happens, Gwen's handwritten text of the *Rede* differs from the text she published in *Green Egg* in only three minor details:

- in couplet #1, there is a dash after the word "must",
- in that same couplet, the word "an" is written as "and", and finally
- in couplet #4 the word "time" is followed not by a comma, but by a dash.

In addition, it is often impossible to tell in Gwen's handwritten text whether she meant to capitalize a word or not.

Rede of the Wiccae

(Being knowne as the counsel of the Wise Ones)

1. **Bide the Wiccan laws ye must
   in perfect love an perfect trust.**

2. **Live an let live -
   fairly take an fairly give.**

3. **Cast the Circle thrice about
   to keep all evil spirits out.**

4. **To bind the spell every time,
   let the spell be spake in rhyme.**

5. **Soft of eye an light of touch -
   speak little, listen much.**

6. **Deosil go by the waxing Moon -
   sing an dance the Wiccan rune.**

7. **Widdershins go when the Moon doth wane,
   an the Werewolf howls by the dread Wolfsbane.**

8. **When the Lady's Moon is new,
   kiss the hand to her times two.**

9. **When the Moon rides at her peak,
   then your heart's desire seek.**

10. **Heed the Northwind's mighty gale -
    lock the door and drop the sail.**

11. When the wind comes from the South,
    love will kiss thee on the mouth.

12. When the wind blows from the East,
    expect the new and set the feast.

13. When the West wind blows o'er thee,
    departed spirits restless be.

14. Nine woods in the Cauldron go -
    burn them quick an burn them slow.

15. Elder be ye Lady's tree -
    burn it not or cursed ye'll be.

16. When the Wheel begins to turn -
    let the Beltane fires burn.

17. When the Wheel has turned a Yule,
    light the Log an let Pan rule.

18. Heed ye flower, bush an tree -
    by the Lady blessed be.

19. Where the rippling waters go,
    cast a stone an truth ye'll know.

20. When ye have need,
    hearken not to other's greed.

21. With the fool no season spend
    or be counted as his friend.

22. Merry meet an merry part -
    bright the cheeks an warm the heart.

23. Mind the Threefold Law ye should -
    three times bad an three times good.

24. When misfortune is enow,
    wear the blue star on thy brow.

25. True in love ever be
    unless thy lover's false to thee.

26. Eight words the Wiccan Rede fulfill -
    an it harm none, do what ye will.

Unfortunately, these differences are so slight that we cannot use them to determine just when Gwen Thompson copied the pages with *The Rede of the Wiccae* that are now in her own *Book*—that is, whether she last copied those pages before or after she sent her article to the editors of *Green Egg*.

When, however, we compare these two texts of the Rede not just with each other, but also with the two earliest available copies of the Rede made by her initiates in 1972 and 1973, then we find one significant difference that allows us to narrow the time frame by a little.

This difference is found in couplet #7, where Gwen's own *Book* and the *Green Egg* text both read:

7.   **Widdershins go when the Moon doth wane,**
     an the Werewolf howls by the dread Wolfsbane.

The 1972 copy, however, reads *Werewolves howl* instead of *Werewolf howls*. Similarly, the 1973 copy reads (ungrammatically) *Werewolves howls*.

These two early initiates made their handwritten copies of Gwen Thompson's own *Book* a few years before she wrote her article for *Green Egg*, and they copied her own *Book* without consulting one another. Each of them meant to copy Gwen's own *Book* faithfully, and—apart from the inevitable individual minor slips of the pen—each of them succeeded in doing so. How, then, can one account for this variant reading that they both have in common? Two slips of the pen cannot easily have happened in just the same way in just the same place in two independent copies; that would be too great a coincidence. The easiest explanation is that they both found this reading in Gwen's own *Book* when they copied it in 1972 and in 1973. Yet it is not in Gwen's own *Book* now. This leads us to conclude that Gwen made a new copy of the pages with the *Rede* for her own *Book* sometime after 1973, and she changed *Werewolves* to *Werewolf* as she did so. When she had made her new copy of the two pages, she destroyed (as was her custom) the old pages that she had copied. On page 53 there is a diagram that shows what happened.

Note, please, that one cannot deduce from this chart alone whether the oldest text of the *Rede* had *Werewolf* or *Werewolves*. Gwen Thompson often recopied parts of her own *Book* during the last decades of her life. It is not at all likely that the pages with the *Rede* that were copied by her early initiates in 1972 and 1973 were the very first copy she had ever made of the *Rede*. It is tedious work to copy and recopy texts by hand. Anyone who has ever done this knows how easy it is to make a mistake, even in a text that one knows by heart, as one's attention wanders for a moment. When one knows the text by heart, one can always restore the correct reading from memory the next time one copies the text.

The Interrelations and Descent of Several Copies of the *Rede of the Wiccae*

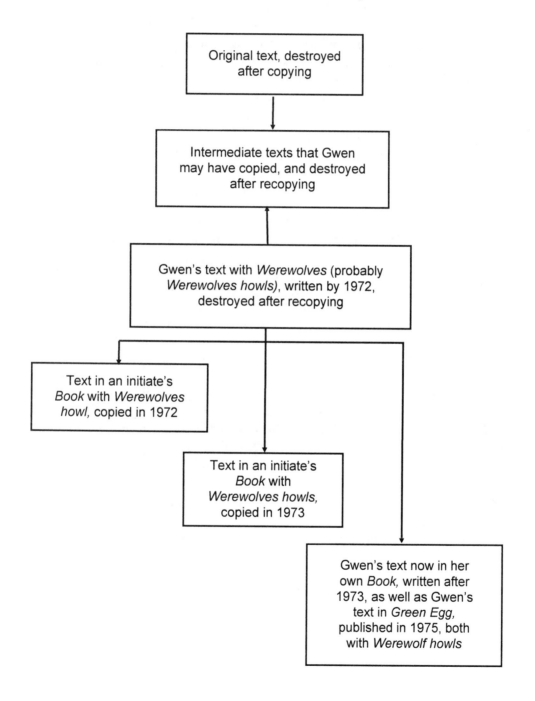

The history of these copies of the *Rede,* therefore, most likely unfolded as follows. In all probability, the *Rede* once had the phrase *Werewolf howls* in couplet #7, as it does today. Sometime before 1972, however, Gwen's attention wandered a little while she was making one more new copy of the *Rede* for her *Book,* so that she accidentally wrote *Werewolves howls* even though it is ungrammatical. In 1972 one early initiate copied this text and unconsciously corrected its grammar, writing *Werewolves howl* in his copy of the *Book.* In 1973 another initiate copied this same text for his copy of the *Book* precisely as he found it, writing *Werewolves howls* despite the bad grammar. Sometime between 1973 and 1975 Gwen herself looked again at those pages in her own *Book,* probably when she was preparing her article for *Green Egg,* and she noticed her mistake. Knowing the *Rede* by heart, she corrected the text from memory to *Werewolf howls* in the typescript that she sent to *Green Egg,* and she also made a new, corrected copy of the *Rede* for her own *Book.* This new, corrected copy is the copy that is in her *Book* today.

Therefore, Gwen Thompson's own last word on the authentic text of the *Rede* is found in her 1975 *Green Egg* article and also on the handwritten pages now in her own *Book.*

In this same article, Gwen Thompson also remarked that "Our own particular *Rede,* however, has appeared within the past year in a perverted form. That is to say, the wording has been changed." She was referring to a different text of her *Rede* that had been recently published in the *Earth Religion News,* volume 1, no. 3 (Spring Equinox, 1974), p. 3, without any commentary.[1] Thereby hangs another tale.

Not all of Gwen Thompson's initiates stayed the course until the end. One of them was the late Ed Buczynski (1947-1989), who studied with Gwen for about two and one-half months, from July to September in 1972. At that time, of course, he made his own copy of the first few dozen pages in Gwen's *Book,* including the *Rede.* Soon after he stopped studying with Gwen, he initiated Herman Slater (1938-1992) into a Coven of his own that he had founded in New York, and this Coven used the parts of Gwen's *Book* that Ed had copied as well as material from other sources. Herman was the publisher of *Earth Religion News,* and Ed was almost certainly the source from whom Herman obtained the *Rede.*

As published in *Earth Religion News,* the *Rede* differs in several places from the texts we have been studying. The greatest difference is in couplets #6-7, which read:

> Deosil go by waxing moon,
> Chanting out the Wiccan rune.

> Widdershins go by waning moon,
> Chanting out the baneful rune.

There is no mention of werewolves at all here, so one cannot easily determine how this text of the *Rede* fits into the history sketched out above.

We shall find it useful to cite the *Earth Religion News* text of the *Rede* at several points in the analysis that follows. However, it was ultimately Gwen's right to say what text of the *Rede* she regarded as authoritative within the Tradition that she founded, and she did so when she published her article in *Green Egg*. It is the latter text on which we shall base our analysis, despite the scraps of evidence we have about older copies of the *Rede* that were formerly in Gwen's own *Book*. These older forms are quite important as witnesses to the earlier history of the text of the *Rede,* and we shall cite them as such. However, history and authority are two quite different things.

First Observations on the Rede

When Robert's attention was first called to Gwen Thompson's *Rede of the Wiccae* by Theitic in the late 1990s, he was already very well acquainted with almost all the books on Witchcraft and Wicca that had been published up to about 1985 by British Witches (such as Gerald Gardner, Justine Glass, Sybil Leek, Doreen Valiente, Janet and Stewart Farrar) and their American adherents (such as Ray Buckland), and also with the descriptions of the markedly different forms of American Witchcraft given by authors Zsuzsanna Budapest, Margot Adler, and Starhawk. As a Medieval philologist, he had also long been critically engaged in the problems raised by Gerald Gardner's claim that his form of Witchcraft and his *Book of Shadows* reached back into the Middle Ages. In this connection he had also carefully examined every published extract from Gardner's *Book of Shadows* and every description of its contents.

The very first thing that struck Robert when he carefully read Gwen Thompson's *Rede* for the first time was how markedly it differed in content from the doctrines and practices of Gardner's Wicca (to the extent that he knew of them as a noninitiate), and indeed from any other form of witchcraft with which he was already familiar from books and articles. To be sure, there were some striking similarities as well, chiefly verbal ones, but it seemed to him that these were mere surface similarities—grace notes, as it were, added to an underlying melody. As he analyzed the *Rede* more fully over the next several years, he found no compelling reason to change his first impression of its text. What now follows are the results of his analysis.

We begin with a few obvious remarks about the form of *Rede.*

The *Rede* consists of 26 rhyming couplets. Each couplet also has a poetic meter, that is, it has a regular pattern of stressed and unstressed syllables. This meter is not the same in all couplets, but varies from one couplet to another.

Many of these 26 couplets seem to belong together as pairs or sets of four, for example, the four couplets about wind blowing from each of the four points of the compass (#10-13), the two couplets about the waxing and the waning moon (#6-7), or the two couplets on Beltane and Yule (#16-17). Other couplets stand alone. These single couplets often seem to have little connection with the couplets that come before and after them, and there may not have been any reason for the particular order in which they stand.

Each individual couplet (or set of linked couplets) is a separate *lore-text,* that is, a brief text that conveys a piece of traditional knowledge or lore in a fixed form. Lore-texts include proverbs, weather rhymes, old sayings whether or not they are in rhyme, and so forth. A *lore-text* has a relatively fixed form of words in which it is handed down from one generation to the next. Although a lore-text can change with time, the change is from one fixed text to another fixed text.

Lore in general, as opposed to lore-texts, can be passed down without any fixed form of words. A traditional dance, for example, is learned by seeing the dance and copying the dancers, not by hearing any fixed form of words. This is important. The history of one or another bit of lore—say, a particular ritual practice—is not the same thing as the history of a specific lore-text about that practice.

Not all fixed texts are lore-texts. There are also short fixed texts used in rituals, which are called *ritual-texts* or ritual phrases (depending on their length). The *Pledge of Allegiance* used in the United States may serve as an example of a secular ritual-text.

Only a few of the couplets in the *Rede* have close parallels with lore-texts or ritual phrases in other Traditions of Witchcraft or Wicca (#1, 6, 23, and 26). Most of the others find their closest parallels in traditional English folklore.

In the following sections we will first examine the metrics of the *Rede,* that is, the poetic form in which it has been composed. Next we will consider its structure and the archaic words and forms in its language. Finally we will investigate the sources, traditional or otherwise, on which it draws. A brief summary of the results will close this part of our work.

The Metrical Form of the *Rede*

As already noted, the *Rede* consists of 26 rhyming couplets. Most of them are in what we shall call *regular meter*. When a couplet is in regular meter, each of its two lines is exactly seven syllables long. In addition, the metrical stresses can fall only on the first, third, fifth, and seventh syllables, not on the second, fourth, and sixth. We write this pattern as [' - ' - ' - '], and we call it the *scansion* of the line.

Here is an example of a couplet in regular meter:

8.	**When the Lady's Moon is new,**	= 7 syllables	[' - ' - ' - ']
	kiss the hand to her times two.	= 7 syllables	[' - ' - ' - ']

Occasionally one of the stresses is missing, usually the second or the third, so that three unstressed syllables follow one after another. Here is an example of a missing stress.

14.	**Nine woods in the Cauldron go -**	= 7 syllables	[' - - - ' - ']
	burn them quick an burn them slow.	= 7 syllables	[' - ' - ' - ']

Rarely there are other, more subtle complications. In the following example it is impossible to say whether the word "desire" is meant to be pronounced in three syllables (de-sigh-er), or whether it is pronounced in two syllables (de-sire) and an illusion of a third, unstressed syllable is automatically created by the two adjacent stressed syllables in the words "desire seek."

9.	**When the Moon rides at her peak,**	= 7 syllables	[' - ' - - - ']
	then your heart's desire seek.	= 7 syllables	[' - ' - ' - ']
		or 6+ syllables	[' - ' - ' 0 ']

(Here the notation "6+ syllables" means that there are only six syllables in the line, but that the two adjacent stressed syllables have created the illusion of a seventh unstressed syllable between them, which is indicated with a "0" in the scansion.)

This illusion of an unstressed syllable between two adjacent stressed syllables is found elsewhere in the *Rede,* for instance:

5.	**Soft of eye an light of touch -**	= 7 syllables	[' - ' - ' - ']
	speak little, listen much.	= 6+ syllables	[' 0 ' - ' - ']

Despite such complications, all of the above couplets count as examples of regular meter. Indeed, 15 out of the 26 couplets are in regular meter: # 5, 8-11, 14-19, 21-24.

Here are the 15 couplets of the *Rede* that are in *regular meter.* Note that many of these couplets go together in obvious pairs, as shown here.

5. Soft of eye an light of touch -
    speak little, listen much.

8. When the Lady's Moon is new,
    kiss the hand to her times two.

9. When the Moon rides at her peak,
    then your heart's desire seek.

10. Heed the Northwind's mighty gale -
    lock the door and drop the sail.

11. When the wind comes from the South,
    love will kiss thee on the mouth.

14. Nine woods in the Cauldron go -
    burn them quick an burn them slow.

15. Elder be ye Lady's tree -
    burn it not or cursed ye'll be.

16. When the Wheel begins to turn -
    let the Beltane fires burn.

17. When the Wheel has turned a Yule,
    light the Log an let Pan rule.

18. Heed ye flower, bush an tree -
    by the Lady blessed be.

19. Where the rippling waters go,
    cast a stone an truth ye'll know.

21. With the fool no season spend
    or be counted as his friend.

22. Merry meet an merry part -
    bright the cheeks an warm the heart.

23. Mind the Threefold Law ye should -
    three times bad an three times good.

24. When misfortune is enow,
    wear the blue star on thy brow.

The other 11 couplets of the *Rede* are in other meters. The most striking of these other meters is found in just two couplets, #2 and #20. Here, although the second

60

line is in regular meter, the first line in only four syllables long, with the stresses on the first and the fourth syllable. We will call this the *short meter*.

2.	Live an let live -	= 4 syllables	[' - - ']
	fairly take an fairly give.	= 7 syllables	[' - ' - ' - ']
20.	When ye have need,	= 4 syllables	[' - - ']
	hearken not to other's greed.	= 7 syllables	[' - ' - ' - ']

Seven other couplets display several kinds of long meter, where one line—in one case, both lines—has eight syllables, with an extra unstressed syllable at the beginning. Two of these couplets form an obvious pair.

1.	Bide the Wiccan laws ye must	= 7 syllables	[' - ' - ' - ']
	in perfect love an perfect trust.	= 8 syllables	[- ' - ' - ' - ']
3.	Cast the Circle thrice about	= 7 syllables	[' - ' - ' - ']
	To keep all evil spirits out.	= 8 syllables	[- ' - ' - ' - ']
4.	To bind the spell every time,	= 8 syllables	[- ' - ' 0 ' (-) - ']
	let the spell be spake in rhyme.	= 7 syllables	[' - ' - '- ']
12.	When the wind blows from the East,	= 7 syllables	[' - ' - ' - ']
	expect the new and set the feast.	= 8 syllables	[- ' - ' - ' - ']
13.	When the West wind blows o'er thee,	= 7 syllables	[' - ' - ' - ']
	departed spirits restless be.	= 8 syllables	[- ' - ' - ' - ']
25.	True in love ever be	= 6+ syllables	[' - ' 0 ' - ']
	unless thy lover's false to thee.	= 8 syllables	[- ' - ' - ' - ']
26.	Eight words the Wiccan Rede fulfill -	= 8 syllables	[- ' - ' - ' - ']
	an it harm none, do what ye will.	= 8 syllables	[- ' - ' - ' - ']

The last of these seven couplets is the only one with exactly eight syllables in each line. The meter of this one couplet we shall call *full long meter;* the meter of the other six couplets will be called *partial long meter*.

The remaining two couplets go far beyond these metrical limits and have lines of nine or even 10 syllables. They are in what we shall call *extra-long meters*. These extra-long meters differ from the regular and long meters not only in length. They also often have two unstressed syllables, not only one or three, to come between successive stressed syllables. This fact gives them a gracefully dancing rhythm that is appropriate to their content, but that is found nowhere else in the *Rede*.

6. **Deosil go by the waxing Moon -**   = 9 syllables   [' - - ' - - ' - ']
    sing an dance the Wiccan rune.   = 7 syllables   [' - ' - ' - ']

7. **Widdershins go when the Moon doth wane,**

             = 9 syllables   [' - - ' - - ' - ']

    an the Werewolf howls by the dread Wolfsbane.

             = 10 syllables   [- - ' - ' - - ' - ']

These two couplets are peculiar in another respect as well. As noted in the previous chapter, they are the only two couplets that are found to differ enormously when Gwen Thompson's version of the *Rede* is compared with the version of the *Rede* published in *Earth Religion News*. Curiously enough, in the *Earth Religion News* version of the *Rede,* these two couplets are much closer metrically to the rest of the *Rede*. Indeed, if "Deosil" were pronounced in the traditional way as "Jessil" (or "Jeshil" or "Dessil") with just two syllables and "Widdershins" were likewise pronounced as "Widd(r)-shins," then these two couplets would be in what we have called regular meter, that is, the most common meter of the *Rede*. However, Gwen Thompson always pronounced these words in three syllables, as "De-o-sil" and "Wid-der-shins."

Deosil go by waxing moon,   = 7 or 8 syllables   ['(-) - ' - ' - ']
Chanting out the Wiccan rune.   = 7 syllables   [' - ' - ' - ']

Widdershins go by waning moon,   = 7 or 8 syllables   ['(-) - ' - ' - ']
Chanting out the baneful rune.   = 7 syllables   [' - ' - ' - ']

Although these metrical differences may seem trivial, hardly worth the reader's attention, nevertheless they will prove to be important later on in the analysis. As we shall see, differences in meter correlate to a large extent with other differences between the various couplets, and will have considerable bearing on the problem of the origin of the *Rede*.

Regular Meter in Spells and Proverbs.

In the English-speaking world, rhyming couplets in *regular meter*—as we have termed it—are traditional for literary representations of spells, as in Shakespeare's *Macbeth*.

Second Witch:

Fillet of a fenny snake,   = 7 syllables   [' - ' - ' - ']
In the caldron boil and bake;   = 7 syllables   [' - ' - ' - ']
Eye of newt, and toe of frog,   (ditto)
Wool of bat, and tongue of dog,

Adder's fork, and blind-worm's sting,   (ditto)
Lizard's leg, and howlet's wing, -
For a charm of powerful trouble,   (ditto)
Like a hell-broth boil and bubble.

All:

Double, double, toil and trouble;   (ditto)
Fire, burn; and caldron, bubble.

Rhyming couplets in this meter, however, are not just a literary convention. They also occur in traditional spells, such as this example (from Isabel Gowdie's *Confession of Witchcraft,* Scotland, 1662) for riding through the air on "windle-straws or bean-stalks":

Horse and hattock, horse and go,	= 7 syllables	[' - ' - ' - ']
Horse and pellatis, ho! ho!²	= 7 syllables	[' - ' - - - ']

For another example, consider the following spell against illness heard by R. M. Heanley in the 1850s, though only published by him many decades later:

Father, Son, and Holy Ghost,	= 7 syllables	[' - ' - ' - ']
Nail the Devil to this post.	= 7 syllables	[' - ' - ' - ']
Thrice I smite with Holy Crok,	= 7 syllables	[' - ' - ' - ']
With this mell I thrice do knock,	= 7 syllables	[' - ' - ' - ']
One for God,	= 3 syllables	[' - ' . . .
and one for Wod,	+ 4 syllables	. . . - ' - ']
and one for Lok.³	+ 4 syllables	. . . - ' - ']

Nor do rhyming couplets in the regular meter occur only in spells. They are also found in proverbs and other kinds of lore-texts. It is here that we find the closest parallels to some of the couplets in the *Rede.*

The following lore-text, for instance, is a piece of proverbial wind-lore from Nova Scotia, where Adriana Porter was born and raised:

When the wind is in the north	= 7 syllables	[' - ' - ' - ']
Dare not go forth.	= 4 syllables	[. . . - ' - ']
When the wind is in the south	= 7 syllables	[' - ' - ' - ']
Blows the bait in the fishes' mouth.	= 8 syllables	[' - ' - - ' - ']
When the wind is in the east	= 7 syllables	[' - ' - ' - ']
'Tis neither fit for man or beast.	= 8 syllables	[- ' - ' - ' - ']
When the wind is in the west	= 7 syllables	[' - ' - ' - ']
Then the weather's always best.⁴	= 7 syllables	[' - ' - ' - ']

63

Compare this with couplets #10-13 of the *Rede:*

10. Heed the Northwind's mighty gale - = 7 syllables   [′ - ′ - ′ - ′]
     lock the door and drop the sail.   = 7 syllables   [′ - ′ - ′ - ′]

11. When the wind comes from the South, = 7 syllables   [′ - ′ - ′ - ′]
     love will kiss thee on the mouth.   = 7 syllables   [′ - ′ - ′ - ′]

12. When the wind blows from the East, = 7 syllables   [′ - ′ - ′ - ′]
     expect the new and set the feast.   = 8 syllables   [- ′ - ′ - ′ - ′]

13. When the West wind blows o'er thee, = 7 syllables   [′ - ′ - ′ - ′]
     departed spirits restless be.   = 8 syllables   [- ′ - ′ - ′ - ′]

The similarities between the two texts are no accident. Clearly the woman who first put together the *Rede* (or at least this part of the *Rede*) knew a proverbial wind text very like the one just quoted, and adapted it to bring out esoteric lore a little more fully.

Note that this particular piece of weather lore is not found only in Nova Scotia, nor is it particularly rare; also, its words are not always and everywhere the same. Here are three other versions of it, some with much less regular meters than the text just quoted:

> When the wind is in the north,
> The skillful fisher goes not forth;
> When the wind is in the east,
> 'Tis good for neither man nor beast;
> When the wind is in the south,
> It blows the flies in the fish's mouth;
> But when the wind is in the west,
> There it is the very best.[5]

> When the wind's in the north,
> Hail comes forth;
> When the wind's in the west,
> Look for a wet blast;
> When the wind's in the soud [= south],
> The weather will be fresh and good;
> When the wind's in the east,
> Cold and snaw comes neist [= next].[6]

> When 't wind's in 't east,
> Cauld and snaw comes 't neist [= next];
> When 't wind's in 't west,
> It suits 't farmer best;

64

When 't wind's in 't north,
We ha' to sup het scalding broth;
When 't wind's in 't south,
It's muck up to 't mouth.[7]

The Structure and Language of the *Rede*

The Structure

The four versions just quoted of this piece of proverbial weather-lore are *composite lore-texts.* That is, each of them is made up of several *simple lore-texts.* In this instance, the simple lore-texts are the *individual* couplets for each of the four winds that blow from the four cardinal points of the compass. The four individual couplets may occur in different orders in different versions of the text (N-S-E-W, N-E-S-W, N-W-S-E and E-W-N-S, in the four versions given above). Each of these couplets can also occur either by itself or, rarely, paired with one other. Thus the antiquary Michael Aislabie Denham collected all of the following separate lore-texts in the first half of the nineteenth century:

When the wind is South,
It blows the bait in the fish's mouth.

When the wind's in the East,
It's neither good for man nor beast;
When the wind's in the South,
It's in the rain's mouth.

When the wind's in the West,
The weather's always best.

When the wind is in the North,
The skillful fisher goes not forth.[8]

To reiterate, it is the individual rhyming couplets that are the primary "building blocks," so to speak, of these *composite lore-texts.* The individual couplets are the *simple lore-texts.* Since they have a common theme, these simple lore-texts can be combined to produce the composite lore-texts just quoted.

Like the texts quoted above, the *Rede* is a *composite lore-text.* However, the *Rede* is a very unusual composite lore-text. For one thing, it has many more parts and is much longer than most composite lore-texts, since it it made up of 26 simple lore-texts. For another thing, the 26 simple lore-texts that it contains are unique ones; that is, not one of them is found with even approximately the same wording anywhere else.

The most natural explanation for these two unusual characteristics of the *Rede* is that it was originally composed by one person who deliberately adapted various shorter lore-texts to suit a common purpose, and did so in writing.

The *Rede,* therefore, is not an oral text, passed from mouth to ear, that just happened to get written down, but it was originally composed in writing, and was the careful work of one person. To be sure, that person took traditional lore-texts as her model and as one of her sources, but she deliberately adapted these sources to serve her own purpose. This purpose is indicated by the title she gave to her composition: she wrote it in order to give *rede* to the *Wiccae.*

The Language

Rede, it must be noted, means counsel or advice, as in the English proverb, "Short rede, good rede."[9] This is an ancient proverb, quoted by a Medieval English chronicler as he narrated the murder of Bishop Walcher of Durham at a council called in 1080 on the pretext of seeking justice for the earlier murder of a man named Ligulf. As reported by Roger of Wendover in 1235, there was neither debate nor trial at this council: one warrior merely cried out, "Short rede, good rede: slay ye the bishop," and they all slew the bishop that very instant.

In the nineteenth century this utterly forgotten proverb was given new life by Sir Walter Scott (1771-1832), who employed it as a deliberate archaism in his novel, *The Fair Maid of Perth* (1828). Sir Walter was one of the first exponents of the Romantic movement in English literature, which created a taste among readers for all things dark, legendary, and magical; and many of his best poems and novels sought to gratify this taste. More than some other Romantic authors, however, Sir Walter had an antiquarian cast of mind. He delighted in finding utterly forgotten English words and phrases and reviving them in his works. It may not be too much to say that he single-handedly launched a fashion for old-fashioned language that is still very much with us today. Not only do Witches and Pagans frequently use such language in their rituals and other oath-bound texts, but anyone who frequents Renaissance Fairs will have heard people—as the quip now goes—"speaking forsoothly." This is a far cry indeed from the genuine spoken (or written) English of the High Middle Ages or the Renaissance.

Indeed, all the other archaic words and forms which the *Rede* contains point to the nineteenth or early twentieth century as the time of its composition. Every one of them is an archaism that had been revived and popularized by Sir Walter Scott or his fellow Romantics, or by some later writer.

It is worth noting that many of these archaic words and forms are used correctly in the *Rede*—although this seems to have been beyond the ability even of many

66

well-educated people who were born after about 1920. (The loss of this ability was probably a consequence of the cultural changes that took the King James version of the Bible, with its archaic English, out of the mainstream of American culture, and have made its language almost incomprehensible now.)

In particular, the archaic pronouns in the *Rede* conform perfectly to the old rules of English grammar (exemplified also by the King James Bible): the forms *thou, thee,* and *thy* are used only for the singular, while *ye* is used only for the nominative plural. Likewise, the archaic conjunction *an* (instead of *if*) is used correctly in couplet #26: an it harm none, do what ye will.[10] (There is no example of the conjunction *an* anywhere in the King James Bible.) A second archaic word not found anywhere in the King James Bible is the preposition *a* (meaning *to*) in couplet # 17.[11]

> 17. **When the Wheel has turned a [= to] Yule,**
>   **light the Log an let Pan rule.**

Verb forms, however, are mostly modern, *begins* instead of *beginneth* in couplet #16, *has* instead of *hath* in couplet #17. Couplet #7, which we have already singled out for special attention a few times, is oddly inconsistent: it has *doth* instead of *does,* but *howls* instead of *howleth.*

> 7. **Widdershins go when the Moon doth wane,**
>   **an the Werewolf howls by the dread Wolfsbane.**

In couplet #4 the verb form *spake* is a genuine old form of the verb *speak* (and it is the norm in the King James Bible, where the principle parts of the verb are *speak, spake, spoken*). Here, however, it is incorrectly used to mean "spoken" instead of "spoke."

> 4. **To bind the spell every time,**
>   **let the spell be spake in rhyme.**

A few other archaic words and forms are also wrongly used. One of these *false archaisms* is the use of the form *ye* instead of *the.* Couplet #15 has both the incorrect use of *ye* (instead of modern *the*) and the correct use of *ye* (instead of modern *you* in the nominative case).

> 15. **Elder be ye [= the] Lady's tree -**
>   **burn it not or cursed ye'll [= you'll] be.**

Ye (instead of *the*), pronounced with an initial *y*-sound, came into use only during the nineteenth century. It arose from a misunderstanding of older English spelling and pronunciation. Originally the definite article *the* was always pronounced with the *th*-sound, just as it is today. However, in the late Middle Ages this word was commonly written *þe,* where the obsolete letter þ (called "thorn") stood for *th*-sound. Handwriting always changes slowly over the centuries, and thus the shape of the handwritten letter þ came more and more to resemble the shape of the handwritten letter *y.* By the middle of the sixteenth century some printers no longer felt any need to have the letter þ in their typecases, but used the letter *y* instead of þ to spell our modern *th* as well as our modern *y.* In this way there arose the spelling *ye* for the definite article *the,* but this did not mark any change in the pronunciation. Once the spelling *ye* had appeared, however, then the definite article *ye* (which was still pronounced with an initial *th*-sound) could not be distinguished in writing from the pronoun *ye* (which had always been pronounced with an initial *y*-sound). As more and more people were taught to read simple texts during the 1800s, they ignorantly supposed that almost all English words were to be pronounced as they were spelled. When such people saw *the* spelled *ye,* they mispronounced it with the *y*-sound. By the end of the nineteenth century two parallel forms of the definite article had been created out of this ignorance: archaic *ye* (always pronounced with the *y*-sound) and common *the* (always pronounced with the *th*-sound). Store signs like "Ye Olde Gifte Shoppe"—when pronounced "yee oldee giftee shoppee"—are the final result of this development. (False pronunciations of this sort, that is, pronunciations that arise from spelling, are also called *spelling pronunciations.*)

By far the most notable of the false archaisms in the *Rede* is the word *Wiccan* in couplets #1, #6, and #26, which Gwen Thompson pronounced as if it was spelled with *ck* instead of *cc.* The form of the word is Old English, and its pronunciation with the *ck*-sound is another spelling-pronunciation, just like in the definite article *ye* instead of *the.*

In the Old English language, long before the Norman Conquest of England, the word for one witch was *wicca* in the masculine gender, but *wicce* in the feminine gender; in the plural, many witches of either gender were *wiccan.* For some centuries before the Norman Conquest the *cc* in these words was pronounced with our modern *tch*-sound (as if they were spelled *witcha, witche,* and *witchan*). The Norman Conquest marked the end of Old English and the beginning of Middle English, with its much simplified grammar and its very different rules of spelling, and so in Middle English a single witch, whether male or female, was a *wicche,* and many witches were *wicchen* or (with a different form of the plural ending) *wicches,* where the *tch*-sound is spelled *cch* (as is usual in Middle English). From these Middle English forms it is only a short jump to the Modern English forms *witch* and *witches.* In Modern English, of course, the *tch*-sound is normally spelled *ch* or *tch.* An un-schooled reader will probably still read the Middle English spelling *cch* with the *tch*-sound, but he would not have any way of knowing that the Old English spelling *cc* represented the same sound. Rather, he would suppose that Old English *cc* was pronounced the same as *cc* in Modern English. This is the source of the modern forms *Wicca* and *Wiccan*, now pronounced with the *ck*-sound instead of the *tch*-sound. In short, they are a false archaism, and the present difference between *Wiccan* and *Witches* is another example of the same process that gave rise to the difference between the false archaism *ye* (pronounced with the *y*-sound) and the common form *the* for the definite article.

The revival of the words *Wicca* and *Wiccan* began with Charles Godfrey Leland, who discussed the Old and Middle English words for witches and wizards in a long footnote in his influential book, *Gypsy Sorcery and Fortune-Telling,* published in 1891.[12] Leland connected these words to a root that meant "to see," "to know" and "to be wise." (His etymology is almost certainly mistaken, according to the best modern specialists in Old English. The root from which the word *wicca* derives is much more likely to have been **weik–* which refers to 'magic and sacred' rather than **weid–* which refers to 'knowledge.') Originally, as with Leland, the forms *wicca* and *wiccan* were revived as nouns for any and all 'witch' and 'witches,' respectively. Later the form *Wiccan*—now with a capital letter—began to be used as an adjective. Even later the noun *Wicca* shifted its meaning from 'a Witch' to 'Witchcraft' (as a religion). The shift was facilitated by Gerald Gardner, who wrote occasionally of "the Wica" (with one *c*) and meant thereby the practitioners of witchcraft as a religion. (Gardner's use was influenced in turn by the earlier revival of another Old English word, *wita,* meaning a council of wise elders.) Whenever one finds the word *Wiccan* used as an adjective in some text, that text—or that variant of the text—cannot have been written before 1891, and it was almost certainly written after 1950.

In the text of the *Rede* the word *Wiccan* is used as an adjective in three couplets (#1, 6, and 26). These couplets, in their present form, cannot easily be assigned to any date before 1950. Its title, *The Rede of the Wiccae,* used the word *Wicca* as a noun meaning 'a witch,' but makes from that word a pseudo-Latin plural, *Wiccae,* as if the word *Wicca* were Latin[!], not Anglo-Saxon.

To sum up the principal results of this section, the *Rede* is a composite lore-text that was composed in writing. Its language, and particularly the specific ways in which archaic and pseudoarchaic words and forms are used, suggests that it was composed no earlier than the nineteenth century. The use of the words *Wicca* and *Wiccan* suggests that the title of the *Rede* and the couplets that contain the latter word (if not the entire *Rede*) were composed in the twentieth century, and most likely in the second half of the twentieth century. If the "Rede" was originally composed in the nineteenth century, then its title and these three couplets (at least) must have been revised or added much later.

A Source Analysis of the *Rede*

As already stated, the *Rede* is largely based on traditional lore, much of which has been adapted to enhance its applicability to Witchcraft and magic. Some of its 26 couplets are strikingly modified versions of traditional lore-texts that have already been recorded and studied by scholars. Other couplets appear not to be derived from any specific lore-text, but put the unspoken lore of traditional rituals and magical practices into memorable words. Only a very few couplets incorporate words, phrases, and sentences that are hallmarks of Gardner's Wicca and the traditions that derive from it. In this section we shall consider each of these three kinds of sources in turn.

Traditional Lore-Texts

As we have already shown, couplets #10-13 of the *Rede* derive from four traditional lore-texts about the four winds. The person who composed the Rede deliberately altered these lore-texts to bring out certain features of magical interest. This is also the case for several other couplets of the *Rede,* which derive in similar ways from traditional mundane lore-texts, generally short proverbs.

Thus for instance, the proverbs "live and let live" and "give and take is fair in all nations" on the one hand, and "need makes greed" on the other, were sources for the two couplets in short meter (#2 and #20).[13]

> 2. **Live an let live -**
>   **fairly take an fairly give.**

> 20. **When ye have need,**
>   **hearken not to other's greed.**

Likewise a proverb such as "hear much, speak little" or "think much, speak little, and write less" was a source for couplet #5, which also draws on the English idioms (that is, fixed phrases) "soft eye and light touch."[14]

> 5. **Soft of eye an light of touch -**
>   **speak little, listen much.**

The same pattern of construction, echoing the idioms "bright cheeks" and "warm heart" while building on the old English greeting "merry meet, merry part," is found in couplet #22.[15]

> 22. **Merry meet an merry part -**
>   **bright the cheeks an warm the heart.**

Merry meet, merry part is well attested as a mundane phrase of greeting and parting from the late seventeenth century onwards. Its reported use by Somerset witches ("A boy! merry meet, merry part," according to the confession of Elizabeth Styles in 1664) simply reflects the common custom of the day, but is one possible source from which Gardner's Wicca drew its well-known ceremonial phrase, "Merry meet and merry part and merry meet again!" where "merry meet again" is understood to refer to the reincarnation of Witches among their loved ones.[16] (Gwen Thompson also understood it to refer to reincarnation.)

A similar mundane, common-sense proverb no doubt underlies couplet #25, though it has not yet been found in any scholarly collection.

> **25. True in love ever be**
> **unless thy lover's false to thee.**

In one case the ultimate sources are not mundane proverbs, but Biblical ones. (In general, memorable Bible verses readily become independent lore-texts, but are not generally included in scholarly collections of proverbs.) Compare couplet #21 with the following three verses from the King James version of the Bible.

> **21. With the fool no season spend**
> **or be counted as his friend.**

He that walketh with wise men shall be wise:
but a companion of fools shall be destroyed.

Let a bear robbed of her whelps meet a man,
rather than a fool in his folly.

Talk not much with a fool,
    and go not to him that hath no understanding:
beware of him,
    lest thou have trouble, and thou shalt never be defiled with his fooleries:
depart from him,
    and thou shalt find rest, and never be disquieted with madness.[17]

Traditional Practices

In other cases, the sources for particular couplets are not so much traditional lore-texts as traditional practices. The most instructive case is that of the paired couplets #16-17:

> **16. When the Wheel begins to turn –**
> **let the Beltane fires burn.**

> **17. When the Wheel has turned a Yule,**
> **light the Log an let Pan rule.**

The first thing that strikes a modern Witch about these couplets is that they cover only two of the eight major stations in the wheel of the year, Beltane and Yule—there is not a word anywhere in the *Rede* about any of the other six, not even the two that are on the other side of the wheel—Hallowe'en across from Beltane, and Midsummer across from Yule. However, just like the *Rede,* the few traditional lore-texts that name more than one of these eight feasts name only Beltane and Yule:

I'll bring your Yule belt to the Beltane bore.[18] [Meaning unclear.]

The fire that's blawn on Beltane e'en may well be black gin Yule.
[The fire that's blown (kindled) on Beltane evening may well be black by Yule.]

A gowk at Yule'll no be bright at Beltane.[19]
[A fool at Yule will not be bright at Beltane.]

This, I think, may be taken as an indication that the author of the *Rede* took a more traditional attitude to the great feasts of the year than do modern Witches. (Indeed, in recent years other Witches have added other couplets to the original text of the *Rede* for the other six great feasts, thereby obscuring the *Rede's* old-fashioned character.)

In fact, the cycle of eight symmetrically placed quarter days and cross-quarter days that is now generally observed by Witches was most probably developed by H. Ross Nichols and Gerald Gardner together during the 1940s.[20]

As to the traditional practices which these couplets embody, both the Beltane fires—often a pair of fires, between which cattle were driven for protection—and the Yule Log are well known ancient practices, and well-documented ones.[21]

Almost as instructive are the paired couplets #14-15.

14. **Nine woods in the Cauldron go -
burn them quick an burn them slow.**

15. **Elder be ye Lady's tree -
burn it not or cursed ye'll be.**

Although in the past a fire was more likely to be built *under* a cauldron than *in* it, nevertheless cauldrons were also used to hold cooking fires aboard wooden ships. Also, fires made of nine woods are a very ancient tradition throughout Europe. (The list of the nine woods to be burned will vary somewhat from one part of Europe to the next, and perhaps also from one occasion to the next.[22]) These ritual fires are often, but not always, kindled as need-fires or neat-fires—an untransmitted fire created for the occasion by the friction of wood rubbing against wood, as by means of a fire-drill—and they were often used to protect cattle from malevolent spellcraft and similar ills. (Among the many older meanings of the word *need* is "tight constraint," as in the friction of wood against wood in a fire-drill; and *neat* is an old word for cattle.) A need-fire made of nine woods has long been a powerful magical artifact.

Moreover, the fact that some woods do indeed burn quickly, while others burn slowly, was still common knowledge in the nineteenth and even the very early twentieth century, when most heating and cooking was still done with fireplaces or wood-burning stoves. This firewood-lore had largely been forgotten by the second half of the twentieth century, once stoves had become gas or electric and fireplaces an ornament rather than a necessity.

Traditionally, the Elder-tree was never one of the nine woods from which such a fire—or any fire—could be made. It was the one tree that must never be felled, cut, broken, or burned on grievous penalty, for instance, on the penalty of being burned out of one's house and home, or seriously injured by one's own ax. Striking, and sometimes even touching, an Elder-tree, whether by accident or on purpose, can also carry a penalty. In old lore, this is because the Elder tree is under the special protection of a personage who is usually called the Devil (who must not be named directly, but is indicated by such terms as "the Old Boy" or "Old Providence"), but also is very rarely said to be an ancient female being ("The Old Lady" or "The Old Girl"). If, indeed, one cannot avoid cutting an Elder-tree, one must say certain words to avert the penalty, for example, "Old Girl, give me of thy wood, and I will give some of mine when I grow into a tree." Thus couplet #15, with its reference to the Lady (rather than to the Old Boy, for instance) gives a rare and arcane piece of traditional tree-lore.[23]

Moon-lore is embodied in another pair of couplets.

8. When the Lady's Moon is new,
   kiss the hand to her times two.

9. When the Moon rides at her peak,
   then your heart's desire seek.

There are many traditional practices when one sees the new moon, but few when one sees the full moon.[24] To kiss one's hand to the moon is an extremely ancient practice, mentioned and condemned in the Bible.

If I beheld the sun when it shined, or the moon walking in brightness;
And my heart hath been secretly enticed, or my mouth hath kissed my hand:
This also were an iniquity to be punished by the judge:
for I should have denied the God that is above.[25]

A rather uncommon form of divination is clearly the subject of couplet #19, although no published work on English folklore seems to mention the practice.

**19. Where the rippling waters go,
     cast a stone an truth ye'll know.**

Couplet #18 is less specific, and simply recommends close attention to the world of plants without mentioning any specific omens that one may draw from them. However, traditional lore mentions many signs and omens that can be taken from plants, and also forms of respect that must be shown to many of them.[26]

**18. Heed ye flower, bush an tree -
     by the Lady blessed be.**

Couplet #24 originally referred to a uncommon form of protective amulet or mark, although once again no published work on English folklore seems to offer more than vague parallels to precisely that practice. There is, however, good evidence for the custom of wearing something blue (usually around the neck or on the head) to protect against misfortune.[27]

**24. When misfortune is enow,
     wear the blue star on thy brow.**

Despite their overtones of magic and divination, these traditional practices were not thought to be particularly esoteric in bygone centuries, but were just part of the common stock of folk magic—what the elite would call the superstitions—that farmers and dairy maids freely used whenever the occasion presented itself. Now, of course, they are no longer matters of common knowledge, although even a century and a half ago they were still thought by many people to be good expressions of traditional lore and wisdom for daily life. In those days, they were almost mundane, though now they have become esoteric.

The Elders of the N.E.C.T.W. would like to add here that initiates understand these couplets to refer to oath-bound practices that go well beyond the mundane folklore cited above.

Practices of Learned Magic

Each of the couplets analyzed so far clearly derives from everyday lore, even if that lore counts as folk magic. However, the *Rede* also contains two couplets that prescribe magical practices of a far less ordinary kind.

**3. Cast the Circle thrice about
     To keep all evil spirits out.**

4. To bind the spell every time,
let the spell be spake in rhyme.

Magic circles to shut out evil are rarely found in English and American folk magic, although sometimes one might plow around one's farm or circumambulate one's house or barn sunwise or deosil, one time or three, for that purpose.[28] These practices go back at least to Classical Antiquity, and maybe far beyond.

Casting or drawing a triple circle, however, may derive from the ceremonial magic of Late Antiquity and the Middle Ages, or perhaps from literary works that portray Medieval or Renaissance magicians at work, where such circles may serve to protect the magician from the spirits he has summoned.[29] A passage from Shakespeare's *Macbeth* may serve as one example.

> The weird sisters, hand in hand,
> Posters of the sea and land,
> Thus do go about, about:
> Thrice to thine and thrice to mine
> And thrice again, to make up nine.
> Peace! the charm's wound up.

A few verses from Samuel Taylor Coleridge's *Kubla Khan* (1816) may serve as another.

> And all who heard should see them there,
> And all should cry, Beware! Beware!
> His flashing eyes, his floating hair!
> Weave a circle round him thrice,
> And close your eyes with holy dread,
> For he on honey-dew hath fed,
> And drunk the milk of Paradise.

Triple Circles of several kinds are also now used by Wiccans in more than one tradition, but much more often to contain the power that has been raised within the Circle than as a defense against evil spirits outside the Circle.[30] This Wiccan practice, however, may derive from the same learned or literary sources, not from folk magic.

Rhymed spells are common in folk magic, though unrhymed spells are also quite common. Couplet #4, however, may also address the creation and design of new spells, or spells for new occasions, and that is a thing very rarely done in traditional folk magic. Rather, it is in fanciful works of literature—often written for children—that new spells seem most often to be created to meet the needs of the plot, and to be created in rhyming form. Gerald Gardner mentions this in his *The Meaning of Witchcraft*: "Mrs. Nesbit wrote many years ago that to work magic you must express your wish in original rhyme made up at the moment . . . "[31] There he also offers his own explanation for the use of rhyme in spell casting. (He is referring to the famous children's author, Edith Nesbit.) A text recently published from Gardner's *Book of Shadows* also recommends the use of rhyme in spells.

Of spells, the exact words matter little if the intent be clear and you raise the true power, and sufficient thereof. Always in rhyme they are. There is something queer about rhyme. I have tried, and the same seem to lose their power if you miss the rhyme. Also in rhyme the words seem to say themselves. You do not have to pause and think: "What comes next?" Doing this takes away much of your intent.[32]

Gwen Thompson, however, understood Couplet #4 as stating an absolute preference for rhymed spells, telling her initiates, "Don't use spells that don't rhyme"—though of course she knew that such spells existed.

Sources in Wicca and Modern Witchcraft

Only five couplets remain, and they are the ones that are most closely connected with Gardner's Wicca and the other traditions of Witchcraft that derive from it. Indeed, three of the five are the only couplets that use the adjective Wiccan.

1. **Bide the Wiccan laws ye must
in perfect love an perfect trust.**

6. **Deosil go by the waxing Moon -
sing an dance the Wiccan rune.**

7. **Widdershins go when the Moon doth wane,
an the Werewolf howls by the dread Wolfsbane.**

23. **Mind the Threefold Law ye should -
three times bad an three times good.**

26. **Eight words the Wiccan Rede fulfill -
an it harm none, do what ye will.**

In Gardner's Wicca, *perfect love* and *perfect trust* are the two verbal passwords that admit the first-degree initiate to the Circle for the first time.[33] To raise power, Wiccans in Gardner's Tradition may dance in a Circle sunwise (deosil) while chanting a poem known as the "Witches' Rune," which he and Doreen Valiente wrote together around 1954 or 1955. The terms *Threefold Law* and *Wiccan Rede* refer to the two main ethical principles of Gardner's Wicca. In October of 1964 Doreen Valiente quoted couplet #26 exactly in her speech at the inaugural dinner of the short-lived Witchcraft Research Association; it seems already to have been current among Witches in England.[33] (In his *Meaning of Witchcraft* (1959), chapter 8, Gardner expressed the same principle in prose: "Do what you like so long as you harm no one.") Even the words *Wicca* and *Wiccan* (which Gwen Thompson pronounced "wicka" and "wickan") seem to have been popularized by Gardner and his early initiates, though they were soon picked up by other traditions.

As for the correlation between werewolves and the herb wolfsbane in couplet #7, it reminds one slightly of a rhyme invented in 1941 by a Hollywood script-writer for the film, *The Wolf Man.*

> Even a man who is pure of heart
> And says his prayers by night
> May become a wolf when the wolfsbane blooms
> And the autumn moon is bright.

However, there is another possibility as well, namely that it refers to the use of wolfsbane (*Aconitum* spp.) in a "flying ointment," that is, an ointment that produces the experience or sensation of flying to a Witches' Sabbat in the form of an animal such as a wolf.[35]

The variant of that pair of couplets (#6+7) published in *Earth Religion News,* however else one may judge it, avoids the problem of a connection between wolfsbane and werewolves, and also is more consistent metrically with the rest of the *Rede.*

> Deosil go by waxing moon,
> Chanting out the Wiccan rune.
>
> Widdershins go by waning moon,
> Chanting out the baneful rune.

Both variants of these couplets reflect the traditional correlation of the waxing moon and deosil circumambulation with generation and increase, and similarly of the waning moon and widdershins circumambulation with corruption and decrease.[36]

The Results of the Analysis

The most striking result of this examination of the form of the *Rede,* its language and its sources, is the fairly strong correlation that appears between all these factors.

Nineteen of the 26 couplets in Gwen Thompson's *Rede* reflect traditional lore and lore-texts that were once the common property of the folk. These traditional lore-texts have been reworded to make them more applicable to magical and esoteric practice, and the unspoken traditional lore has been put into words to create new lore-texts that have the same form (rhyming couplets) as the others. Fourteen of the 19 couplets in this group are in what we have called regular meter. Twelve of these

14 make natural pairs (#8+9, 10+11, 14+15, 16+17, 18+19, 21+22). The other two stand by themselves (#5 and 24). (Only one couplet outside this group has regular meter.) Two of the remaining five couplets in this group are the only two couplets in short meter (#2 and 20). The last three couplets in this group are in long meter, and two of them make another natural pair (#12+13, 25). We shall call these 19 couplets the *traditional core* of the *Rede*.

Four of the remaining seven couplets are in long meter, and one in regular meter. Two of them are the two couplets that probably derive from accounts of magic in popular works of imaginative literature (#3-4); they form a natural pair in long meter. We shall call them the *literary group*.

The other two couplets in long meter (#1 and 26) use the false archaism *Wiccan* and strongly echo Gardner's form of Wicca. They are the first and last couplets in the *Rede*, and they form a frame around the rest of the *Rede*. We shall call them the *frame*. Like the frame couplets, the one remaining couplet in regular meter (#23) also strongly echoes Gardner's form of Wicca. We shall group these three couplets together as the *Wiccan group*, and in a moment we shall add one more couplet to that group.[37]

The last two couplets (#6+7) are particularly problematic. These are the two that show far and away the greatest variation in the five sources that we have used. They are the two that differ the most in their metrical form—extra-long meter—from the rest of the *Rede*. One of them (#6) uses the false archaism *Wiccan*, and so we will add it to the Wiccan group. The other (#7) is the only couplet that has an internal inconsistency in its use of archaic grammar (*howls* versus *doth*), and the only one that mentions a magical relationship (between wolfsbane and werewolves) that has little basis whatsoever either in traditional English lore or in the literature of magic and occultism. We shall call these two couplets the *problem* couplets.

The results of this analysis are shown in summary form in the table on page 78. In this table, couplets that make natural pairs are linked by the plus sign (+), whether they occupy one line or two in the table. From this table we can formulate a reasonable theory about the composition of the *Rede of the Wiccae*.

Most of the *Rede*, including all of the couplets in the core group, is clearly the work of a single hand. This person drew on various traditional lore-texts, common proverbs and idioms, and traditional practices to create a long, composite lore-text containing at least 19 couplets. All of these couplets were meant to be in the meter traditionally used for spells and proverbs, which we have called *regular meter*, although one pair of couplets (to judge by their present wording) ended up with one extra unstressed syllable at the beginning of the second line, yielding one form of long meter. This person almost certainly worked in writing, for the composite lore-text that resulted is longer than any known oral composite lore-text in English. We shall call this person, for want of a better term, the *first hand* of the *Rede.*

The first hand knew a lot of traditional English lore, but none of it was specifically agricultural lore. If one can identify the first hand's home at all, it was a place where sailing ships were part of daily life, like Salem or Marblehead or Yarmouth. (Compare the references to dropping the sail in couplet #10 and to building a fire *in* a cauldron in couplet #14.) The first hand had no difficulty at all in using archaic English pronouns such as thee and ye correctly, which suggests that she was most likely born sometime before about 1930 at the latest. The first hand had no knowledge whatsoever of Gardner's Wicca or any of its texts and distinctive practices. Indeed, there is no way to tell just from this part of the *Rede* whether the first hand even called herself a Witch specifically, or thought of her lore as Witchcraft. These 19 couplets do not have a particularly "witchy" tone, though they are very well-rooted in English traditional folk magic.

Couplet(s)	Meter	Source	Feature	Group
# 1	Long	Wiccan	Frame	Wiccan group
# 2	Short	Proverbs		**Core group***
# 3 + 4	Long	Literary		*Literary group*
# 5	Regular	Proverbs and idioms		**Core group**
# 6 +	Extra-Long	Lore and Wiccan	Problem	Wiccan groups
# + 7	Extra-Long	Lore and fanciful	Problem	
# 8 + 9	Regular	Lore		**Core group**
# 10 + 11	Regular	Lore-texts		**Core group**
# 12 + 13	Long	Lore-texts		**Core group**
# 14 + 15	Regular	Lore (traditional practices)		**Core group**
# 16 + 17	Regular	Lore (traditional practices)		**Core group**
# 18 + 19	Regular	Lore (traditional practices)		**Core group**
# 20	Short	Proverb		**Core group**
# 21 +	Regular	Proverbs (Biblical proverbs)		**Core group**
# + 22	Regular	Ritual phrase and idioms		**Core group**
# 23	Regular	Wiccan		Wiccan group
# 24	Regular	Lore (Traditional practices)		**Core group**
# 25	Long	Proverb?		**Core group**
# 26	Long	Wiccan	Frame	Wiccan group

*Couplets in bold face are the work of the first hand. The other couplets are the work of the second hand, except for #3 + 4, which might be the work of either.

It is impossible to tell, from the texts now available, whether the 19 couplets in the core group originally followed one another in the order in which they now stand. However, most of the couplets form natural pairs (with the same long meter in couplets #12+13, #24+25). It is obvious that the two isolated couplets in short meter (#2 and 20) have similar content and would form another natural pair if only they had been placed next to one another. The other isolated couplet (#5) might even form a natural triplet with one of the pairs (#24+25). It is very tempting to speculate that the first hand designed her 19 couplets so that most of them would form nine natural pairs, and that a few of her couplets were later rearranged by another hand.

In any event, it is necessary to posit that some other person has revised the work of the first hand, if our analysis has been correct so far and if what we have said about the first hand is also correct. If these things are so, then several couplets in the *Rede* cannot have been composed by the first hand. These are the couplets:

- that break the metric patterns of the traditional core,
- that employ archaic language imprecisely or incorrectly,
- that use the false archaism *Wiccan* (pronounced "wick-an" by Gwen), and
- that display familiarity with Gardner's Wicca and its close relatives.

The kind of Wicca that Gardner publicized in his writings from 1949 onward, and a few other related traditions of Witchcraft, crossed the Atlantic only in the 1960s. In those years several English Witches made long visits to the United States, or even (like Ray Buckland and later Sybil Leek) settled there permanently. At the same time a few American Witches subscribed to some of the English periodicals devoted to Witchcraft (like *The Pentagram*). There is no evidence that there were any initiates into Gardner's Wicca or any of its close relatives anywhere in North America before about 1959, or in the United States before about 1961.[38]

By these criteria, five couplets (#1, 6+7, 23, and 26) cannot be the work of the first hand, namely, the two *frame couplets*, the two *problem couplets*, and the one other that is part of the *Wiccan group*. The person who added these five couplets to the *Rede*, and perhaps rearranged its traditional core a little, we shall call the *second hand* of the *Rede*. The two *problem* couplets (#6+7) show more textual instability than any other part of the *Rede*, and may have been the very last couplets to reach their present and final form. (The second hand also is responsible for the present title of the *Rede*, for the same reasons.)

It is unclear whether the two couplets that we have termed the *literary group* (#3+4) are the work of the first hand or the second. The probabilities seem more or less equally balanced on either side.

If the above analysis is accurate, then the *Rede of the Wiccae* is the work of two distinct people, one probably much older than the other. The older one built on English traditional lore; the younger one drew from Wicca and Witchcraft as they had taken shape after about 1950. Nothing prevents us from identifying the younger of these two people as Gwen Thompson herself, though she did not tell her initiates that she took any part in the composition of the *Rede*.

Since the second hand (most likely Gwen Thompson) revised the *Rede* sometime during the 1960s, it is not at all difficult to explain how the last couplet in the *Rede* is identical with a couplet quoted by Doreen Valiente in England in 1964. The 1960s were a decade when English and American traditions of Wicca and Witchcraft flowed freely back and forth across the Atlantic, and influenced one another. It is hard to tell, at this far a remove, whether Doreen had seen a copy of Gwen's *Rede* by 1964, or whether Gwen had heard of Doreen's speech before she finished revising the *Rede* sometime in the 1960s, but we may be sure that at least one of these two things happened.

The fact that the last couplet is the one and only couplet in the *Rede* in full long meter suggests that Gwen borrowed it from an outside source (if not directly from Doreen Valiente) and added it to the other couplets. Indeed, those two lines may have inspired her to revise the material that she had inherited from the first hand, and to give the resulting text its present title, for the word rede itself is found only in that last couplet and in the title, nowhere else in the text.

However, it is the older of these two people—the first hand—who interests us the most in our investigation. If the above analysis is correct, then one cannot just dismiss Gwen's grandmother tale out of hand. Instead, one must critically examine every aspect of that tale to discern what kernels of truth may lie hidden within it. That will be the task of the next and last part of this book.

Endnotes

1. It may be found reprinted in Appendix E.

2. Her confessions were published by Robert Pitcairn. *Criminal Trials in Scotland, from AD 1488 to AD 1624.* Edinburgh: Maitland Club, 1833; 3 vols., III, p. 602-18.

3. R. M. Heanley, "The Vikings: Traces of their Folklore in Marshland," *Saga-Book of the Viking Club* 3 (1901-1903): 35-62 [p. 52-54 where the actions are also described that must accompany the spell].

4. Helen Creighton. *Bluenose Magic: Popular Beliefs and Superstitions in Nova Scotia.* Toronto: The Ryerson Press, 1968, p. 250.

5. H. H. C. Dunwoody. *Weather Proverbs,* (U.S. War Department, Signal Service Notes, no. IX). Washington, D.C.: Government Printing Office, 1883, p. 85.

6. Michael Aislabie Denham. *A Collection of Proverbs and Popular Sayings Relating to the Seasons, the Weather, and Agricultural Pursuits; Gathered Chiefly from Oral Tradition.* Publications of the Percy Society, 20/3. London: The Percy Society (1847): 18.

7. Michael Aislabie Denham. *The Denham Tracts: A Collection of Folklore,* James Hardy, ed. London: The Folklore Society, 1892, 1895; 2 vols. [original editions self-published, 1846-1859], II, p. 23.

8. Michael Aislabie Denham. *A Collection of Proverbs and Popular Sayings Relating to the Seasons, the Weather, and Agricultural Pursuits; Gathered Chiefly from Oral Tradition.* Publications of the Percy Society, 20/3 London: The Percy Society (1847): 10, 12, and 17.

9. William George Smith. *The Oxford Dictionary of English Proverbs,* 2nd ed. rev., by Paul Harvey. Oxford: Clarendon Press, 1948, p. 585. This source will be abbreviated as ODEP in all other endnotes.

10. Elsewhere in the *Rede* the word *an* means *and.*

11. Both of these nonbiblical archaisms were used by Sir Walter Scott.

12. Charles Godfrey Leland. *Gypsy Sorcery and Fortune-Telling.* New York: Charles Scribner's Sons, 1891, p. 66.

13. ODEP, p. 376, 238, and 446.

14. ODEP, p. 286-87 and 650.

15. ODEP, p. 421.

16. Ronald Hutton. *The Triumph of the Moon: A History of Modern Pagan Witchcraft*. Oxford: Oxford University Press, 1999, p. 56, points to a Freemasonic parallel from around 1800: "Happy have we met, Happy have we been, / Happy may we part, And happy meet again." The Freemasonic reference is not to reincarnation, but to the next meeting of the Lodge.

17. Proverbs 13:20, 17:12 and Ecclesiasticus 22:13.

18. Michael Aislabie Denham. *The Denham Tracts: A Collection of Folklore*, James Hardy, ed. London: The Folklore Society, 1892, 1895; 2 vols. [original editions self-published, 1846-1859], II, p. 92.

19. The *Oxford English Dictionary*, s. v. "Beltane" (these two examples are from the years 1835 and 1862).

20. Ronald Hutton. *The Triumph of the Moon: A History of Modern Pagan Witchcraft*. Oxford: Oxford University Press, 1999, p. 233-36 and 246-48. Philip Carr-Gomm. *In the Grove of the Druids: The Druid Teachings of Ross Nichols*. London: Watkins, 2002, p. 1-20.

21. Ronald Hutton. *The Stations of the Sun: A History of the Ritual Year in Britain*. Oxford: Oxford University Press, 1996, p. 38-41 and 218-25.

22. Here too other Witches have added nine other couplets to the original *Rede*, one for each of the nine woods that they have supposed must be used. There are now versions of the *Rede* with as many as 18 added couplets (yielding a total of 44 couplets in all).

23. R. M. Heanley. "The Vikings: Traces of their Folklore in Marshland," *Saga-Book of the Viking Club* 3 (1901-1903): 35-62 [at 55-57]. Also see Katharine Briggs, *An Encyclopedia of Fairies, Hobgoblins, Brownies, Bogies, and Other Supernatural Creatures*. New York: Pantheon Books, 1976, p. 316 and Iona Opie and Moira Tatem. *A Dictionary of Superstitions*. Oxford, New York: Oxford University Press, 1989, p. 137-39. In the following endnotes these two volumes will be cited as EF and DS, respectively.

24. DS, p. 279-83, also 260-66, and 252 for an example of mirror divination at the full moon to see one's future husband.

25. Job 31:26-28.

26. DS, p. 163-64 and 443-44 on white flowers; EF, p. 159-61 on fairy trees.

27. DS, p. 33.

28. DS, p. 383-86.

29. Richard Kieckhefer. *Forbidden Rites: A Necromancer's Manual of the Fifteenth Century*. University Park, Penn.: Pennsylvania State University Press, 1997, p. 170-85 and plates.

30. Gerald Gardner. *Witchcraft Today*. London: Rider, 1954, p. 26, specifies the dimensions of such a triple Circle.

31. Gerald Gardner. *The Meaning of Witchcraft*. London: Aquarian, 1959, p. 101.

32. Aidan A. Kelly. *Crafting the Art of Magic, Book I: A History of Modern Witchcraft, 1939-1964*. St. Paul, Minn.: Llewellyn, 1991, p. 81.

33. They may also have been used as passwords in Freemasonry from time to time, though we are unable to cite a published source.

34. Extensive extracts from her speech were published in the account of this dinner, "Fifty at 'Pentagram' Dinner," *Pentagram* 2 (November 1964): 1-3. Also see Hans Holzer. *The Truth About Witchcraft* New York: Doubleday, 1969, p. 127-29, where the article is summarized and the couplet quoted again.

35. Margaret Murray. *The Witch Cult in Western Europe*. Oxford: Oxford University Press, 1921, p. 279-80; and Alexander Kuklin. *How Do Witches Fly: A Practical Approach to Nocturnal Flights*. Mountain View, Calif.: AceN Press, 1999.

36. DS, p. 260-64 and 383-86.

37. One might ask whether couplet #18 should be assigned to the Wiccan group also, because of the phrase "blessed be." This phrase is often understood in Wicca to be an abbreviation of the words that accompany the ritual action known as the Five-fold Kiss. See Aidan A. Kelly. *Crafting the Art of Magic, Book I: A History of Modern Witchcraft, 1939-1964*. St. Paul, Minn.: Llewellyn, 1991, p. 52, 123; Janet and Stewart Farrar. *A Witches Bible Compleat*. New York: Magickal Childe, 1984, I, p. 40-41, 172; II, p. 17-18, 30. However, the same phrase "blessed be" is also often found in the King James Bible, so the question remains an open one.

38. In 1961 or 1962 Robert heard from two of his women friends that a Witch living in Berkeley, California, was teaching Witchcraft (to adults only). His friends did not know her name, but knew how to get in touch with her, and would have done so if only they had been over 21 at the time. At that time Robert was a freshman or sophomore at the University of California in Berkeley, and his friends in Berkeley High School were a year or two younger than he. Neither he nor his friends ever learned more about this at the time, but decades later,

in the 1990s, Robert happened to meet another person who had been a senior in Berkeley High School at the time, and told her this story. She responded that her English teacher during her senior year (1960/61) had been a visiting teacher from England, a very striking red-haired woman, and she had often told her class that she was a Witch. Robert thinks that this visiting teacher, whose name his friend could not remember, may have been the Witch who offered classes in Witchcraft in 1961. This visiting English teacher may also have been the Witch who stands at the head of the lineage of the so-called "Central Valley" covens in California, which do not descend from Ray Buckland and his wife, but have much the same practices and oath-bound texts, and are known to descend from some other Witch whose name no living person remembers.

Part 5

Conclusion

Gwen Thompson's Grandmother Tale Revisited

We have finally arrived at the end of our labor, and one question still remains. Now that we know so much about Adriana Porter and about the *Rede of the Wiccae,* what can we say about Gwen Thompson's grandmother tale? Is it entirely fictional, like many other tales about grandmothers who were traditional witches? Could it be entirely true, just as Gwen told it? Or is it a mixture of truth and falsehood—or, to use less pointed terms, a blend of real memories, wishful thinking, and romantic fancy?

In her article in *Green Egg,* Gwen Thompson said that her grandmother was named Adriana Porter. This is true. She said that Adriana Porter had "crossed over into the Summerland" in 1946, when she "was well into her nineties." Her grandmother did indeed die in 1946, although she was only 88 years old at the time. Gwen, however, may not have known her grandmother's year of birth exactly.

In the same article, Gwen Thompson described herself as "a Traditionalist, versed in lore taken from certain Witches of the British Isles." She said that "our own particular form of the Wiccan *Rede* . . . was passed on to her heirs by Adriana Porter," and that the text given in her article was its "original form." Finally, she mentioned that "a perverted form" of that *Rede* had recently been published, that is, one in which "the wording has been changed." The reader is left to infer—for Gwen does not say it in so many words—that the "certain Witches of the British Isles" from whom she received her Tradition were her ancestors, not Witches in twentieth-century England. This would be a natural enough inference in light of what Gwen says about Adriana Porter as her source for the *Rede,* but it is still just an inference.

In short, Gwen's words about her grandmother and the *Rede* were either written in a careless or unclear fashion, or they were—please forgive the pun—a fine and *crafty* piece of wordsmanship that suggests something without actually saying it.

The mundane details in the grandmother tale that Gwen Thompson told to her initiates can be confirmed, for the most part, by mundane sources, except in one respect. Gwen told her initiates or let them believe that quite soon after her father's death her mother had remarried, converted to a conservative form of Protestant Christianity, broke with Gwen's grandmother's Witchcraft, and thereafter kept Gwen from her grandmother. However, the published Directories and Poll Tax Lists for the town of Melrose show that Gwen's mother and grandmother continued to share the same house at 76 First Street until 1941, for an entire decade after her father's death in 1931.[1] After that year Gwen's grandmother lived in Fitch Home, a home for the elderly, but at the same time Gwen's mother took new lodgings only a few blocks from Fitch Home. Gwen's mother married again only in 1945, when Gwen was already in her late teens, only a year before Gwen's grandmother died. If Gwen continued to live with her mother—a detail that cannot be ascertained from the Directories and Poll Tax Lists—then this part of her grandmother tale is something other than the literal truth. In that case, it may reflect Gwen's attitude toward her mother, which was not a friendly one during the years when her initiates knew her. We hope that further research may shed more light on this.

In any event, we cannot judge the truth of a tale only by the form and manner in which it has been told. It is a great fault of human nature that people confuse sincerity with truth, and insincerity with falsehood. A sincere person may be sincerely mistaken, and even an insincere person may speak the truth when it seems convenient. Truth and sincerity are two wholly different things, as are insincerity and falsehood. It is important to remember this as one tries to assess the value of ancestral tales and family traditions, whether mundane or magical.

Keeping this in mind, can we get behind the form and manner of Gwen Thompson's grandmother tale to her grandmother as a real person? Can we find any kernels of truth in her tale? To some slight extent we can, though our harvest of truth will be a meager one.

We have argued that the *Rede,* as published by Gwen Thompson, is the work of two people, the first of whom was older than the second, and who had finished her couplets before the second began to work. We have also managed to say a little about each of these two people.

What little we could say about the older person is fully consistent with what we now know about Adriana Porter. It is nowhere near enough to prove that she actually was Adriana Porter; but if she was not Adriana herself, she was probably a person of the same generation or older who grew up in a seaport such as Yarmouth.

The younger of these two people can only have been Gwen Thompson herself. She might have rearranged the 19 couplets (or 21, if we include the literary group) that came down to her from the older person. She certainly added seven (or five) further couplets, some of which she had composed herself—though with far less skill than the older person. She may have borrowed one of these couplets (#26) from an outside source such as Doreen Valiente.

Any reader who accepts our conclusions both gains and loses. The gain is that our conclusions seem to support Gwen Thompson's account of her grandmother as a person with a strong interest in magical folklore, whether or not she thought of it as Witchcraft or called herself a Witch. The loss is that Gwen was stretching the truth when she said that the text which she published was the "original form" of the *Rede* as it had come down to her from Adriana Porter. (If the published text is the unaltered original text of the *Rede,* then the *Rede* cannot have been written until some years after Adriana Porter had died. If, on the other hand, the text of the *Rede* was revised at some point prior to publication, then the published text cannot be the original form of the *Rede.* The reader cannot have it both ways at once without rejecting the entire analysis that we have presented in Part 4 of this book.)

We are of the opinion that the greater part of the *Rede*—19 or 21 of its 26 couplets—was indeed passed down to Gwen Thompson from Adriana Porter, just as Gwen said. We are also of the opinion that Gwen revised Adriana Porter's work in the 1960s, adding seven or five other couplets (and perhaps rearranging the ones that she had inherited) that resonated more closely with other contemporary forms of Witchcraft and Wicca.

In Part 3, we showed that Adriana Porter had the resources and opportunities to become well acquainted with a number of alternative, magical new religious movements, and also with various forms of occultism and esotericism, during the last 40 or 50 years of her long life. We also pointed out that her younger years had been spent in a world rich in all sorts of folklore, including superstitions, folk magic, and tales about ghosts and witches. All this merely raised a possibility. If, however, the core group of couplets in the *Rede* were her work, then this is no longer just a possibility. It has almost become a certainty.

Finally, what can we say about Gwen Thompson's claim of an ancestral tradition of Witchcraft that went back beyond Adriana Porter through her mother, Sarah Arnot Cook, and her grandmother, Wealthy Trask, to Somerset County, England, in the seventeenth century? These two women were indeed Adriana

Porter's mother and grandmother, and her Trask ancestors did indeed immigrate to New England from Somerset County in the seventeenth century.

Moreover, people were indeed executed for the crime of witchcraft in Somerset County in the seventeenth century, which was also home to many cunning-men and cunning-women in later centuries.[2] However, none of these witches or cunning-folk seem to have had the surname Trask, and there is no known genealogical connection between any of them and the Trask family. (Of course, only a few of their names appear in the published records.) Nor were the Trasks or any of their close kin accused of the crime of witchcraft at Salem in 1692. In short, there is no ancient evidence whatever to support even a suspicion that any of these Trasks were either witches (as defined in the laws of that time) or Witches (as the term is now used). However, there is also no good evidence against Gwen Thompson's claim—nor could there be, in the nature of things.

If ancient evidence is lacking, however, there remains the far more recent evidence of the *Rede* and of Gwen Thompson's entire oath-bound *Book,* which (she claimed) was a record of her ancestral Tradition of Witchcraft. Theitic is willing to state here—without going into the details—that the Witchcraft in the *Book* seems to him to have been blended with popular occultism and esotericism from the nineteenth and twentieth centuries. Only an initiate could analyze the entire *Book* using the methods that we have applied to the *Rede* here, and only through such an analysis could one hope to determine whether it was Gwen herself who was responsible for this blend, or Adriana Porter, or both. Gwen's own account of how she turned her grandmother's legacy, a bundle of loose papers, into the *Book* some time after 1946 leaves plenty of room for conjecture about this.

As for the *Rede* itself, our analysis suggests that most of it is the work of one of Gwen's ancestors. Most likely this was her grandmother, though one or another of her grandmother's close relatives cannot entirely be ruled out. There seems to be nothing in the *Rede* that unambiguously points back to a time before the 1800s. Our verdict so far about Gwen's claim of a deep ancestral Tradition of Witchcraft must be the Scottish one, *not proven.*

However, not all ancestral traditions have to be deep ones. It is not too hard to find and document families, at least in North America, that have sustained a general interest in all kinds of alternative religions, in occultism and esotericism, and in folk-magic through several generations for a century or more. One may loosely term them "esoteric families," that is, families in which a taste for such things has been handed down from parents to children (often, from mothers to daughters only) for several generations.[3] In many parts of the United States (at least), such families have long been able to find books and teachers in order to satisfy their taste for all these things, as our historical summary in Part 3 has shown. The evidence presented in this book strongly suggests that Adriana Porter's family, in Massachusetts and perhaps also in Nova Scotia, was such an "esoteric family."

Now the words *witch* and *witchcraft* have always conveyed exciting hints of both danger and power to women. It is also not too difficult to find women who on occassion spoke proudly of women as witches, and who referred to women's special powers—especially over men—as witchcraft. In short, the strategic use of these words can be a way for a woman to claim special power precisely because she is a woman. (Of course, it became relatively safe to make this claim only once women were no longer imprisoned and executed for witchcraft.) On page 42 we cited the example of Emma Hardinge Britten, a Spiritualist and occultist who made just this claim during the second half of the nineteenth century.

Moreover, toward the end of the nineteenth century English folklorists began to speculate that the witches of bygone centuries may actually have been the last adherents of a pre-Christian religion, whether Druidry or some other kind of Paganism.[4] These speculations soon entered the sphere of public discourse. The publication of Gerald Gardner's two quasianthropological books on Witchcraft in the 1950s seems only to have added fuel to an already burning fire. From this time onward, the words *Witch* and *Witchcraft*—now capitalized!—serve two purposes at once: they were used not only to claim special power for oneself (as formerly), but also to characterize and legitimize one's alternative religion or spirituality.

Thus any girl born into such an "esoteric family" during the twentieth century might easily have developed an interest in Witchcraft (or in Wicca) and eventually have decided to call herself a Witch. It seems likely that Gwen Thompson did just that.

Nor is it wholly impossible that some of that girl's women ancestors might also have called themselves witches—if not Witches—at least on occasion, as a way to claim special power for themselves as women. It is just possible that Adriana Porter was such a woman.[5] Further than this the evidence does not permit us to go.

In summary, then, the available evidence supports just two modest conclusions.

First, we have shown that *The Rede of the Wiccae* in 26 couplets (see pages 50-51) was a part of Gwen Thompson's *Book* by the very early 1970s. The text of the *Rede* that she published in *Green Egg* in 1975 and that is now also in her *Book* is the earliest and most authoritative text of the *Rede* now extant. (We make an exception for the single couplet quoted by Doreen Valiente in 1964 and published in *Pentagram* in the same year, which we suppose Gwen incorporated into her *Rede* from an earlier source.) All other texts of the *Rede* known to the authors of this book clearly derive from Gwen's text. This includes the variant published in *Earth Religion News* in 1974 and all the variants with more than 26 couplets.

The *Rede of the Wiccae,* moreover, is the work of two hands, Gwen's and another's. The other hand most likely is that of her grandmother, Adriana Porter; if it is not, it is the hand of some person very like Adriana Porter, belonging to the same generation and having the same background.

Second, we have *not* shown that Gwen Thompson inherited an ancient ancestral Tradition of Witchcraft, as she claimed. But we have found support for a plausible claim of a far more general character, namely, that she came from a family that had had an interest in occultism, esotericism, and magical folklore for at least two generations before her.

These two generations were, of course, the only ones with whom Gwen Thompson had been in close contact as a child growing up in her grandmother's house. However, her father and grandfather died when Gwen was very young, and her grandmother died when Gwen was in her late teens. Soon thereafter her mother remarried. All that Gwen may have had to build on, when Gerald Gardner's books on Wicca and Witchcraft first appeared in the 1950s, were her memories of a happier childhood and of a trunk with an old bundle of loose papers inside. When she decided to go public as a Witch, this was the ground on which she staked her claim within that new religious movement.

However, the faculty of memory is highly creative, and no memory is ever wholly free of the distorting touch of fear and desire. Wishful thinking and fancy have shaped many a fond memory. Old papers, too, are often ambiguous and hard to interpret when taken out of their original context. In such circumstances, Gwen could have told her grandmother tale in utter sincerity and been sincerely mistaken as to certain of its details, even details to which we would ascribe the greatest importance.

Or perhaps not. Perhaps Gwen Thompson exemplified Gardner's maxim that we quoted in the beginning of this book: "Witches are consummate leg-pullers; they are taught it as part of their stock-in-trade."[6]

In the end, Gwen Thompson's sincerity is far less important than whatever truth can be extracted from her grandmother tale. Robert and Theitic are confident that they have begun to do just that. They also hope that they have broken a trail which someday others will turn into a high road leading to a greater understanding of the historical roots of her Tradition of Witchcraft, however old they may be and however deep they may run. It is her Tradition of Witchcraft—however one may value it or whatever its origin may in fact have been—that is Gwen Thompson's own last best legacy to the generations that will follow her.

Endnotes

1. A nearly complete file of these *Directories* and *Poll Tax Lists* is available in the Melrose Public Library.

2. Joseph Glanvill. *Sanducismus Triumphatus, or Full and Plain Evidence Concerning Witches and Apparitions,* 3rd ed. London: S. Lownds, 1689, p. 344-72, gives many seventeenth-century cases. Also see Owen Davies, *A People Bewitched: Witchcraft and Magic in Nineteenth Century Somerset.* Bruton, Somerset: Bruton Press, 1999, for later cunning folk in Somerset county.

3. In much the same way, one often speaks of "Freemasonic families," that is, families in which most adult males have been Freemasons and an interest in Freemasonry has been handed down from fathers to sons for a number of generations.

4. Ronald Hutton. *The Triumph of the Moon: A History of Modern Pagan Witchcraft.* Oxford: Oxford University Press, 1999, chapters 7-8.

5. Adriana Porter (1857-1946) was a generation younger than Emma Hardinge Britten (1823-1899).

6. It is Robert's firm opinion that there is the closest possible connection in human nature between genuine, inspired religious or spiritual teaching, on the one hand, and great skill in the art of deception, on the other. Each requires an unusual degree of empathy and attention and a profound knowledge of the human condition. Neither con artists nor religious teachers appreciate the close kinship between their different callings, but it seems to him to be a fact of human nature nonetheless.

Appendices

Appendix A
Genealogical Tables Showing
Adriana Porter's Ancestry

The following tables have been designed to summarize Adriana Porter's ancestry back to her first ancestors who immigrated to New England in the 1600s, and to show the best genealogical sources for each ancestor.

The reader unaccustomed to genealogical charts may find them somewhat difficult to use at first. The following remarks are meant as a guide.

Chart #0 shows, moving in three columns from left to right, the two parents, the four grandparents and the six known great-grandparents of Adriana Porter. (She had eight great-grandparents, but two of them have not yet been identified.) In each couple, the wife is given first, then the husband, so the uppermost lines reading across each chart are the umbilical lines (i.e., show matrilineal descent).

For each couple, the dates and places of birth, marriage, and death are given, when they are known or can be reasonably inferred. Below each person, in angled brackets <>, are cited our sources of information. These sources are abbreviated, but the abbreviations are expanded into full references in Appendix B.

The ancestry of five of Adriana Porter's great-grandparents is also known, and is given in charts #1 through 4 (on her mother's side) and chart #8 (on her father's side). The ancestry of her sixth known great-grandparent, Mary Tardy, which is given in Chart #7, was discovered only recently, and has not yet been traced back to all her first immigrant ancestors.

Charts #1-4 and #8 give, as just said, the ancestry of five of Adriana Porter's eight greatgrandparents. They have the same structure as Chart #0. Thus they indicate her lines of descent for three more generations backward, to her great-great-great-great-grandparents.

In many cases the ancestry of these great-great-great-great-grandparents can be traced back one, two, or three further generations to the very first generation of settlers in New England. These additional lines of descent can be found on the charts that have numbers such as #1a, 1b, 1c, etc., and immediately follow the charts numbered #1, #2, #3, etc. (English ancestors of the first immigrants are not given here.)

Note how each chart is linked to the ones that precede and follow it logically by notes such as [⟶ #1] or [⟵ #1a].

Note, too, that superscript numerals after given names show the generation of each person, counting forward from the earliest immigrant ancestor with the same surname. The names of all immigrant ancestors have been underlined.

An index of all persons named in these charts will be found in Appendix C.

Chart 0

Immediate Ancestry of Adriana Porter
(1857-1946)
of
Yarmouth, Nova Scotia,
and
Melrose, Massachusetts

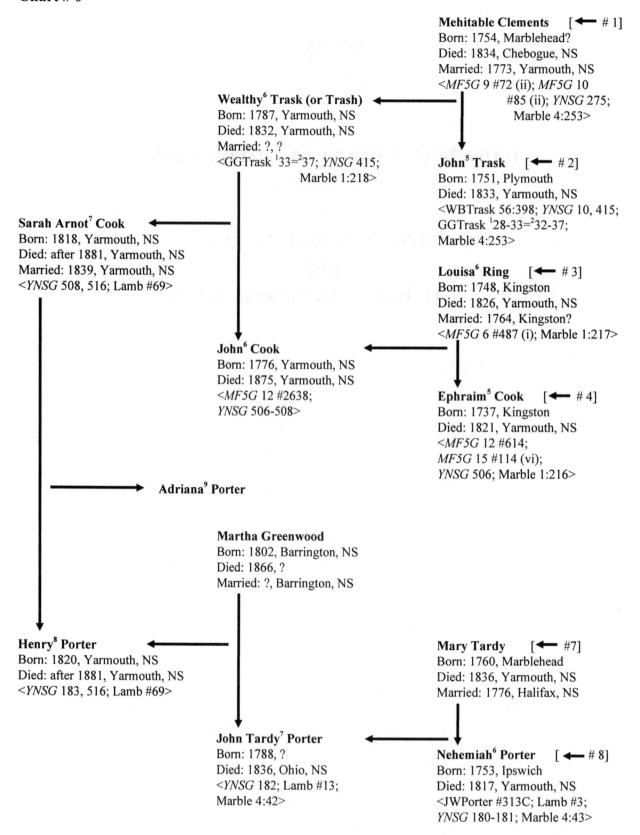

Mehitable Clements   [⬅ # 1]
Born: 1754, Marblehead?
Died: 1834, Chebogue, NS
Married: 1773, Yarmouth, NS
<*MF5G* 9 #72 (ii); *MF5G* 10
            #85 (ii); *YNSG* 275;
        Marble 4:253>

Wealthy⁶ Trask (or Trash)
Born: 1787, Yarmouth, NS
Died: 1832, Yarmouth, NS
Married: ?, ?
<GGTrask ¹33=²37; *YNSG* 415;
        Marble 1:218>

John⁵ Trask   [⬅ # 2]
Born: 1751, Plymouth
Died: 1833, Yarmouth, NS
<WBTrask 56:398; *YNSG* 10, 415;
GGTrask ¹28-33=²32-37;
Marble 4:253>

Sarah Arnot⁷ Cook
Born: 1818, Yarmouth, NS
Died: after 1881, Yarmouth, NS
Married: 1839, Yarmouth, NS
<*YNSG* 508, 516; Lamb #69>

Louisa⁶ Ring   [⬅ # 3]
Born: 1748, Kingston
Died: 1826, Yarmouth, NS
Married: 1764, Kingston?
<*MF5G* 6 #487 (i); Marble 1:217>

John⁶ Cook
Born: 1776, Yarmouth, NS
Died: 1875, Yarmouth, NS
<*MF5G* 12 #2638;
YNSG 506-508>

Ephraim⁵ Cook   [⬅ # 4]
Born: 1737, Kingston
Died: 1821, Yarmouth, NS
<*MF5G* 12 #614;
MF5G 15 #114 (vi);
YNSG 506; Marble 1:216>

Adriana⁹ Porter

Martha Greenwood
Born: 1802, Barrington, NS
Died: 1866, ?
Married: ?, Barrington, NS

Henry⁸ Porter
Born: 1820, Yarmouth, NS
Died: after 1881, Yarmouth, NS
<*YNSG* 183, 516; Lamb #69>

Mary Tardy   [⬅ #7]
Born: 1760, Marblehead
Died: 1836, Yarmouth, NS
Married: 1776, Halifax, NS

John Tardy⁷ Porter
Born: 1788, ?
Died: 1836, Ohio, NS
<*YNSG* 182; Lamb #13;
Marble 4:42>

Nehemiah⁶ Porter   [⬅ # 8]
Born: 1753, Ipswich
Died: 1817, Yarmouth, NS
<JWPorter #313C; Lamb #3;
YNSG 180-181; Marble 4:43>

Charts 1 and 1a - 1e

Ancestry of Mehitable Clements
(1754-1834)
of
Essex County, Massachusetts,
and
Yarmouth County, Nova Scotia

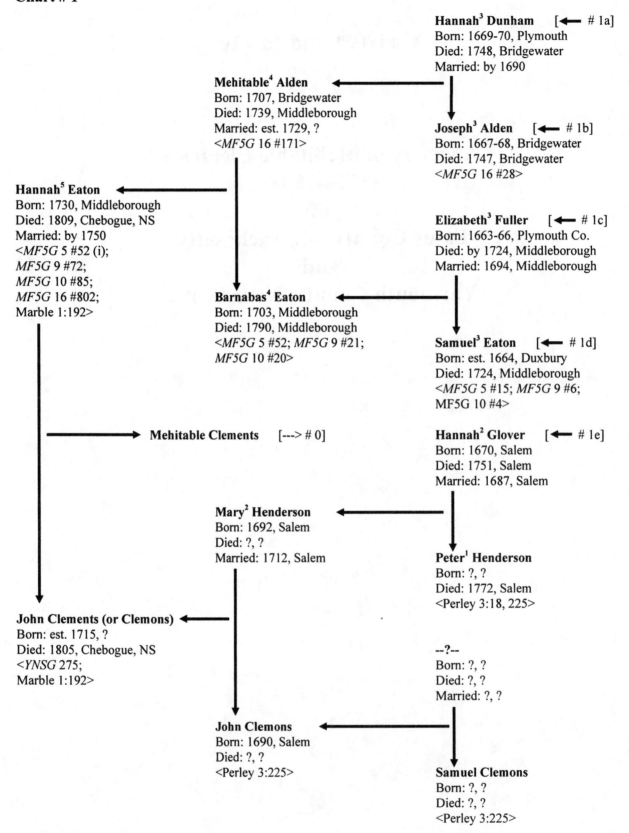

Hannah³ Dunham   [← # 1a]
Born: 1669-70, Plymouth
Died: 1748, Bridgewater
Married: by 1690

Mehitable⁴ Alden
Born: 1707, Bridgewater
Died: 1739, Middleborough
Married: est. 1729, ?
<*MF5G* 16 #171>

Joseph³ Alden   [← # 1b]
Born: 1667-68, Bridgewater
Died: 1747, Bridgewater
<*MF5G* 16 #28>

Hannah⁵ Eaton
Born: 1730, Middleborough
Died: 1809, Chebogue, NS
Married: by 1750
<*MF5G* 5 #52 (i);
MF5G 9 #72;
MF5G 10 #85;
MF5G 16 #802;
Marble 1:192>

Elizabeth³ Fuller   [← # 1c]
Born: 1663-66, Plymouth Co.
Died: by 1724, Middleborough
Married: 1694, Middleborough

Barnabas⁴ Eaton
Born: 1703, Middleborough
Died: 1790, Middleborough
<*MF5G* 5 #52; *MF5G* 9 #21;
MF5G 10 #20>

Samuel³ Eaton   [← # 1d]
Born: est. 1664, Duxbury
Died: 1724, Middleborough
<*MF5G* 5 #15; *MF5G* 9 #6;
MF5G 10 #4>

Mehitable Clements   [---> # 0]

Hannah² Glover   [← # 1e]
Born: 1670, Salem
Died: 1751, Salem
Married: 1687, Salem

Mary² Henderson
Born: 1692, Salem
Died: ?, ?
Married: 1712, Salem

Peter¹ Henderson
Born: ?, ?
Died: 1772, Salem
<Perley 3:18, 225>

John Clements (or Clemons)
Born: est. 1715, ?
Died: 1805, Chebogue, NS
<*YNSG* 275;
Marble 1:192>

--?--
Born: ?, ?
Died: ?, ?
Married: ?, ?

John Clemons
Born: 1690, Salem
Died: ?, ?
<Perley 3:225>

Samuel Clemons
Born: ?, ?
Died: ?, ?
<Perley 3:225>

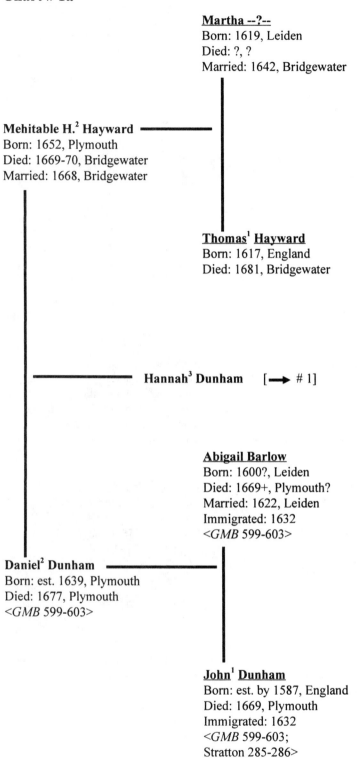

Martha --?--
Born: 1619, Leiden
Died: ?, ?
Married: 1642, Bridgewater

Mehitable H.[2] Hayward
Born: 1652, Plymouth
Died: 1669-70, Bridgewater
Married: 1668, Bridgewater

Thomas[1] Hayward
Born: 1617, England
Died: 1681, Bridgewater

Hannah[3] Dunham   [➝ # 1]

Abigail Barlow
Born: 1600?, Leiden
Died: 1669+, Plymouth?
Married: 1622, Leiden
Immigrated: 1632
<GMB 599-603>

Daniel[2] Dunham
Born: est. 1639, Plymouth
Died: 1677, Plymouth
<GMB 599-603>

John[1] Dunham
Born: est. by 1587, England
Died: 1669, Plymouth
Immigrated: 1632
<GMB 599-603;
Stratton 285-286>

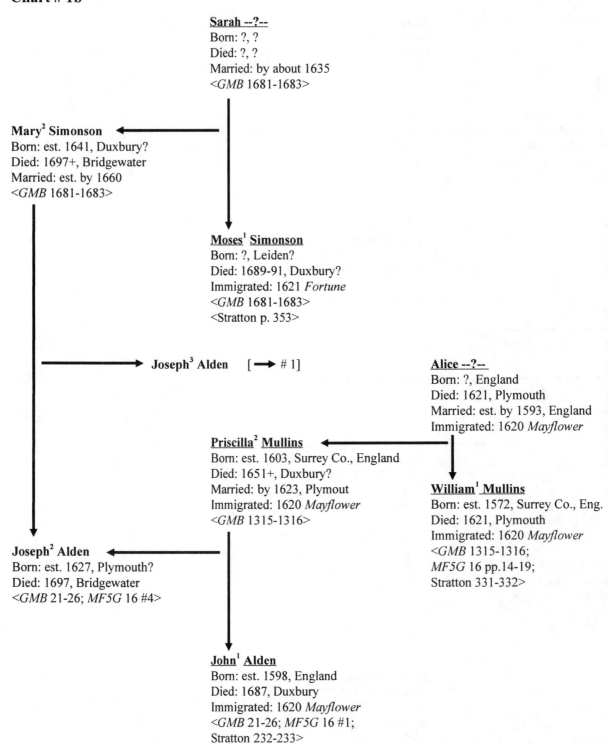

Sarah --?--
Born: ?, ?
Died: ?, ?
Married: by about 1635
<*GMB* 1681-1683>

Mary² Simonson
Born: est. 1641, Duxbury?
Died: 1697+, Bridgewater
Married: est. by 1660
<*GMB* 1681-1683>

Moses¹ Simonson
Born: ?, Leiden?
Died: 1689-91, Duxbury?
Immigrated: 1621 *Fortune*
<*GMB* 1681-1683>
<Stratton p. 353>

Joseph³ Alden   [➔ # 1]

Alice --?--
Born: ?, England
Died: 1621, Plymouth
Married: est. by 1593, England
Immigrated: 1620 *Mayflower*

Priscilla² Mullins
Born: est. 1603, Surrey Co., England
Died: 1651+, Duxbury?
Married: by 1623, Plymout
Immigrated: 1620 *Mayflower*
<*GMB* 1315-1316>

William¹ Mullins
Born: est. 1572, Surrey Co., Eng.
Died: 1621, Plymouth
Immigrated: 1620 *Mayflower*
<*GMB* 1315-1316;
MF5G 16 pp.14-19;
Stratton 331-332>

Joseph² Alden
Born: est. 1627, Plymouth?
Died: 1697, Bridgewater
<*GMB* 21-26; *MF5G* 16 #4>

John¹ Alden
Born: est. 1598, England
Died: 1687, Duxbury
Immigrated: 1620 *Mayflower*
<*GMB* 21-26; *MF5G* 16 #1;
Stratton 232-233>

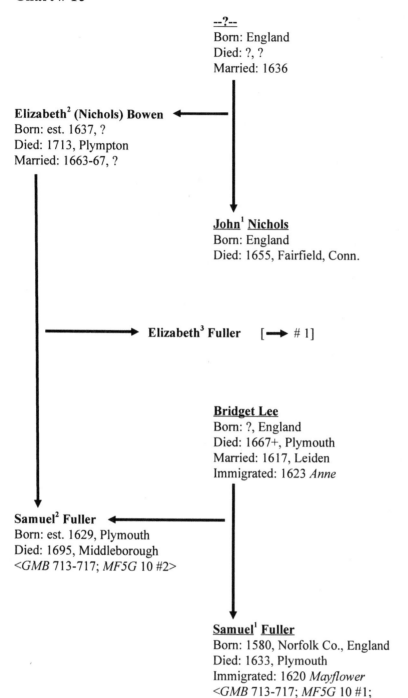

--?--
Born: England
Died: ?, ?
Married: 1636

Elizabeth² (Nichols) Bowen ◄
Born: est. 1637, ?
Died: 1713, Plympton
Married: 1663-67, ?

John¹ Nichols
Born: England
Died: 1655, Fairfield, Conn.

Elizabeth³ Fuller   [➤ # 1]

Bridget Lee
Born: ?, England
Died: 1667+, Plymouth
Married: 1617, Leiden
Immigrated: 1623 *Anne*

Samuel² Fuller ◄
Born: est. 1629, Plymouth
Died: 1695, Middleborough
<*GMB* 713-717; *MF5G* 10 #2>

Samuel¹ Fuller
Born: 1580, Norfolk Co., England
Died: 1633, Plymouth
Immigrated: 1620 *Mayflower*
<*GMB* 713-717; *MF5G* 10 #1;
Stratton 295>

103

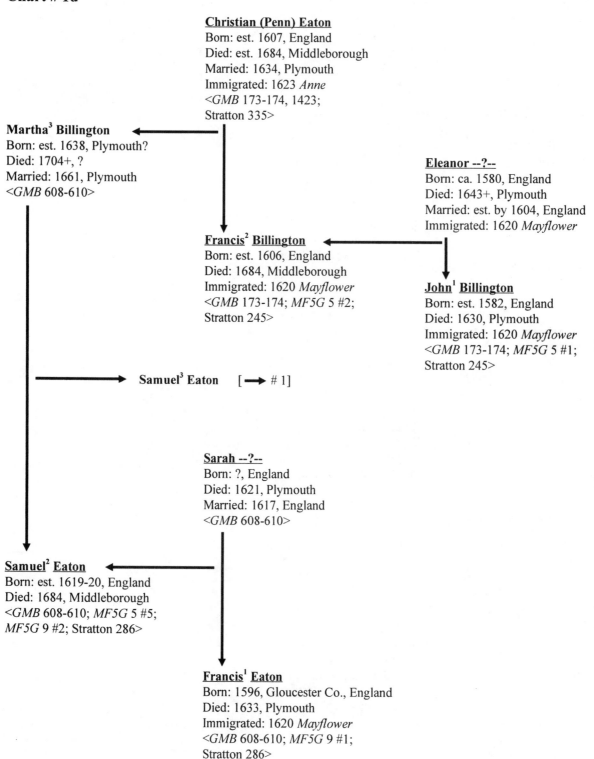

Christian (Penn) Eaton
Born: est. 1607, England
Died: est. 1684, Middleborough
Married: 1634, Plymouth
Immigrated: 1623 *Anne*
<*GMB* 173-174, 1423;
Stratton 335>

Martha³ Billington
Born: est. 1638, Plymouth?
Died: 1704+, ?
Married: 1661, Plymouth
<*GMB* 608-610>

Eleanor --?--
Born: ca. 1580, England
Died: 1643+, Plymouth
Married: est. by 1604, England
Immigrated: 1620 *Mayflower*

Francis² Billington
Born: est. 1606, England
Died: 1684, Middleborough
Immigrated: 1620 *Mayflower*
<*GMB* 173-174; *MF5G* 5 #2;
Stratton 245>

John¹ Billington
Born: est. 1582, England
Died: 1630, Plymouth
Immigrated: 1620 *Mayflower*
<*GMB* 173-174; *MF5G* 5 #1;
Stratton 245>

Samuel³ Eaton   [➝ # 1]

Sarah --?--
Born: ?, England
Died: 1621, Plymouth
Married: 1617, England
<*GMB* 608-610>

Samuel² Eaton
Born: est. 1619-20, England
Died: 1684, Middleborough
<*GMB* 608-610; *MF5G* 5 #5;
MF5G 9 #2; Stratton 286>

Francis¹ Eaton
Born: 1596, Gloucester Co., England
Died: 1633, Plymouth
Immigrated: 1620 *Mayflower*
<*GMB* 608-610; *MF5G* 9 #1;
Stratton 286>

Ancestry of Adriana Porter
Chart # 1e

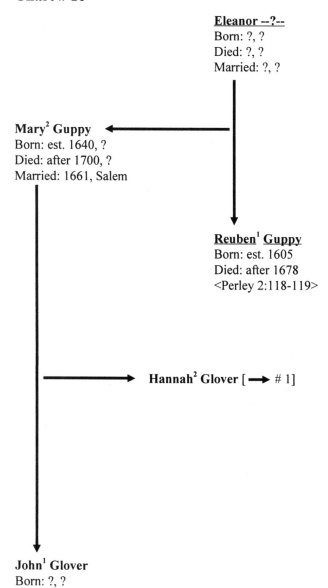

Eleanor --?--
Born: ?, ?
Died: ?, ?
Married: ?, ?

Mary² Guppy
Born: est. 1640, ?
Died: after 1700, ?
Married: 1661, Salem

Reuben¹ Guppy
Born: est. 1605
Died: after 1678
<Perley 2:118-119>

Hannah² Glover [➡ # 1]

John¹ Glover
Born: ?, ?
Died: 1695, Salem
<Perley 2: 118-119; 3:18>

Charts 2 and 2g - 2h

Ancestry of John[5] Trask
(1751-1833)
of
Plymouth County, Massachusetts,
and
Yarmouth County, Nova Scotia

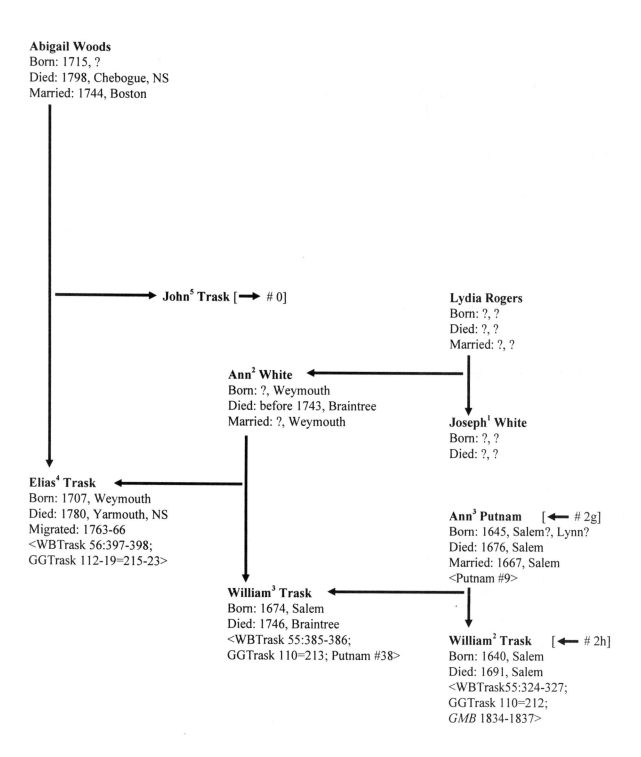

Abigail Woods
Born: 1715, ?
Died: 1798, Chebogue, NS
Married: 1744, Boston

John⁵ Trask [➡ # 0]

Lydia Rogers
Born: ?, ?
Died: ?, ?
Married: ?, ?

Ann² White
Born: ?, Weymouth
Died: before 1743, Braintree
Married: ?, Weymouth

Joseph¹ White
Born: ?, ?
Died: ?, ?

Elias⁴ Trask
Born: 1707, Weymouth
Died: 1780, Yarmouth, NS
Migrated: 1763-66
<WBTrask 56:397-398;
GGTrask 112-19=215-23>

Ann³ Putnam   [⬅ # 2g]
Born: 1645, Salem?, Lynn?
Died: 1676, Salem
Married: 1667, Salem
<Putnam #9>

William³ Trask
Born: 1674, Salem
Died: 1746, Braintree
<WBTrask 55:385-386;
GGTrask 110=213; Putnam #38>

William² Trask   [⬅ # 2h]
Born: 1640, Salem
Died: 1691, Salem
<WBTrask55:324-327;
GGTrask 110=212;
GMB 1834-1837>

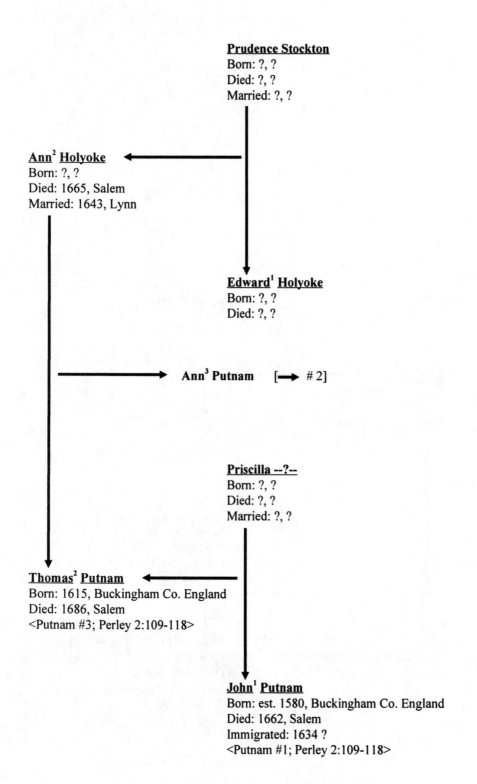

Prudence Stockton
Born: ?, ?
Died: ?, ?
Married: ?, ?

Ann² Holyoke
Born: ?, ?
Died: 1665, Salem
Married: 1643, Lynn

Edward¹ Holyoke
Born: ?, ?
Died: ?, ?

Ann³ Putnam   [➔ # 2]

Priscilla --?--
Born: ?, ?
Died: ?, ?
Married: ?, ?

Thomas² Putnam
Born: 1615, Buckingham Co. England
Died: 1686, Salem
<Putnam #3; Perley 2:109-118>

John¹ Putnam
Born: est. 1580, Buckingham Co. England
Died: 1662, Salem
Immigrated: 1634 ?
<Putnam #1; Perley 2:109-118>

<u>**Sarah --?--**</u>
Born: ?, ?
Died: after 1666
Married: by 1634, Salem?

William^2 Trask   [➡ # 2]

<u>**William^1 Trask**</u>
Born: 1585, East Coker, Somerset Co. England
Died: 1666, Salem
Immigrated: 1624 *Zouche Phenix*
<*GMB* 1834-1837;
WBTrask 53:43-53; 54:279-283; 55:321;
GGTrask 13-9=23-11>

**Ancestry of Louisa[6] Ring
(1748-1826)
of
Plymouth County, Massachusetts,
and
Yarmouth County, Nova Scotia**

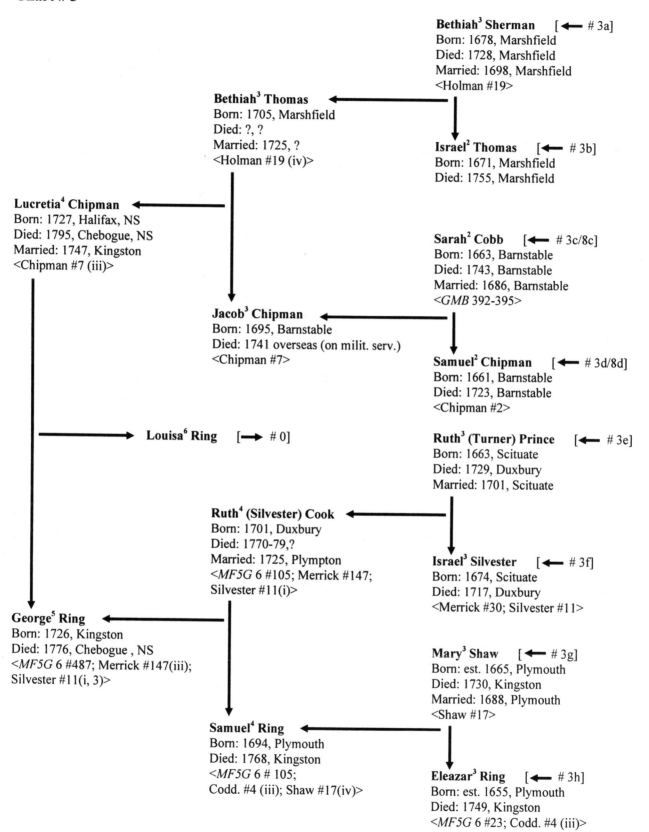

Bethiah³ Sherman   [← # 3a]
Born: 1678, Marshfield
Died: 1728, Marshfield
Married: 1698, Marshfield
<Holman #19>

Bethiah³ Thomas
Born: 1705, Marshfield
Died: ?, ?
Married: 1725, ?
<Holman #19 (iv)>

Israel² Thomas   [← # 3b]
Born: 1671, Marshfield
Died: 1755, Marshfield

Lucretia⁴ Chipman
Born: 1727, Halifax, NS
Died: 1795, Chebogue, NS
Married: 1747, Kingston
<Chipman #7 (iii)>

Sarah² Cobb   [← # 3c/8c]
Born: 1663, Barnstable
Died: 1743, Barnstable
Married: 1686, Barnstable
<*GMB* 392-395>

Jacob³ Chipman
Born: 1695, Barnstable
Died: 1741 overseas (on milit. serv.)
<Chipman #7>

Samuel² Chipman   [← # 3d/8d]
Born: 1661, Barnstable
Died: 1723, Barnstable
<Chipman #2>

Louisa⁶ Ring   [→ # 0]

Ruth³ (Turner) Prince   [← # 3e]
Born: 1663, Scituate
Died: 1729, Duxbury
Married: 1701, Scituate

Ruth⁴ (Silvester) Cook
Born: 1701, Duxbury
Died: 1770-79,?
Married: 1725, Plympton
<*MF5G* 6 #105; Merrick #147;
Silvester #11(i)>

Israel³ Silvester   [← # 3f]
Born: 1674, Scituate
Died: 1717, Duxbury
<Merrick #30; Silvester #11>

George⁵ Ring
Born: 1726, Kingston
Died: 1776, Chebogue , NS
<*MF5G* 6 #487; Merrick #147(iii);
Silvester #11(i, 3)>

Mary³ Shaw   [← # 3g]
Born: est. 1665, Plymouth
Died: 1730, Kingston
Married: 1688, Plymouth
<Shaw #17>

Samuel⁴ Ring
Born: 1694, Plymouth
Died: 1768, Kingston
<*MF5G* 6 # 105;
Codd. #4 (iii); Shaw #17(iv)>

Eleazar³ Ring   [← # 3h]
Born: est. 1655, Plymouth
Died: 1749, Kingston
<*MF5G* 6 #23; Codd. #4 (iii)>

Ancestry of Adriana Porter
Chart # 3a

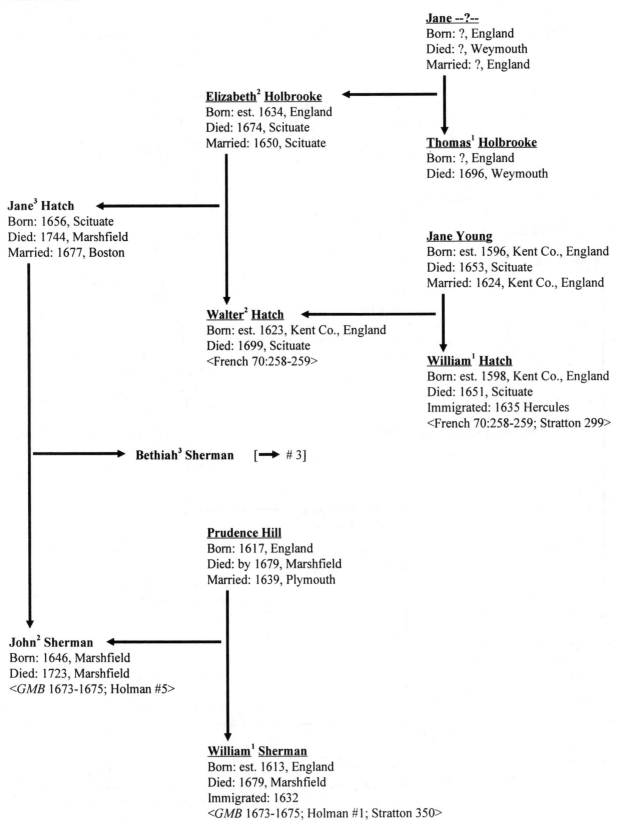

Jane --?--
Born: ?, England
Died: ?, Weymouth
Married: ?, England

Elizabeth² Holbrooke
Born: est. 1634, England
Died: 1674, Scituate
Married: 1650, Scituate

Thomas¹ Holbrooke
Born: ?, England
Died: 1696, Weymouth

Jane³ Hatch
Born: 1656, Scituate
Died: 1744, Marshfield
Married: 1677, Boston

Jane Young
Born: est. 1596, Kent Co., England
Died: 1653, Scituate
Married: 1624, Kent Co., England

Walter² Hatch
Born: est. 1623, Kent Co., England
Died: 1699, Scituate
<French 70:258-259>

William¹ Hatch
Born: est. 1598, Kent Co., England
Died: 1651, Scituate
Immigrated: 1635 Hercules
<French 70:258-259; Stratton 299>

Bethiah³ Sherman   [→ # 3]

Prudence Hill
Born: 1617, England
Died: by 1679, Marshfield
Married: 1639, Plymouth

John² Sherman
Born: 1646, Marshfield
Died: 1723, Marshfield
<*GMB* 1673-1675; Holman #5>

William¹ Sherman
Born: est. 1613, England
Died: 1679, Marshfield
Immigrated: 1632
<*GMB* 1673-1675; Holman #1; Stratton 350>

112

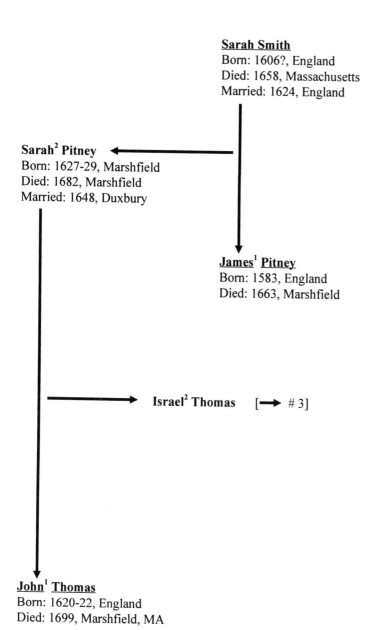

Sarah Smith
Born: 1606?, England
Died: 1658, Massachusetts
Married: 1624, England

Sarah^2 Pitney
Born: 1627-29, Marshfield
Died: 1682, Marshfield
Married: 1648, Duxbury

James^1 Pitney
Born: 1583, England
Died: 1663, Marshfield

Israel^2 Thomas   [➔ # 3]

John^1 Thomas
Born: 1620-22, England
Died: 1699, Marshfield, MA

Ancestry of Adriana Porter
Chart # 3c = # 8c

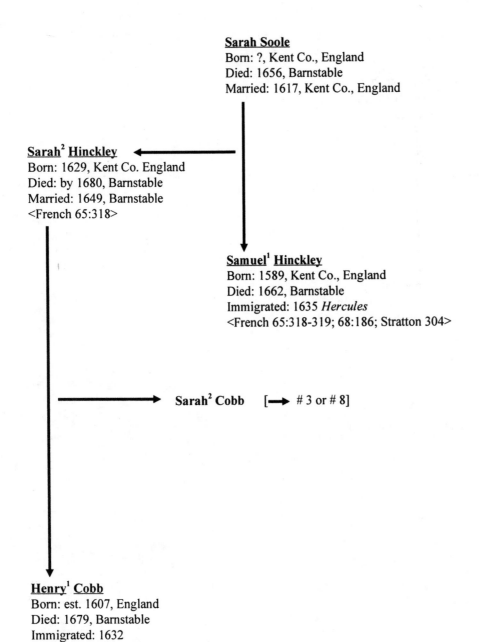

Sarah Soole
Born: ?, Kent Co., England
Died: 1656, Barnstable
Married: 1617, Kent Co., England

Sarah[2] Hinckley
Born: 1629, Kent Co. England
Died: by 1680, Barnstable
Married: 1649, Barnstable
<French 65:318>

Samuel[1] Hinckley
Born: 1589, Kent Co., England
Died: 1662, Barnstable
Immigrated: 1635 *Hercules*
<French 65:318-319; 68:186; Stratton 304>

Sarah[2] Cobb   [→ # 3 or # 8]

Henry[1] Cobb
Born: est. 1607, England
Died: 1679, Barnstable
Immigrated: 1632
<*GMB* 392-395; Stratton 265-266>

Ancestry of Adriana Porter
Chart # 3d = # 8d

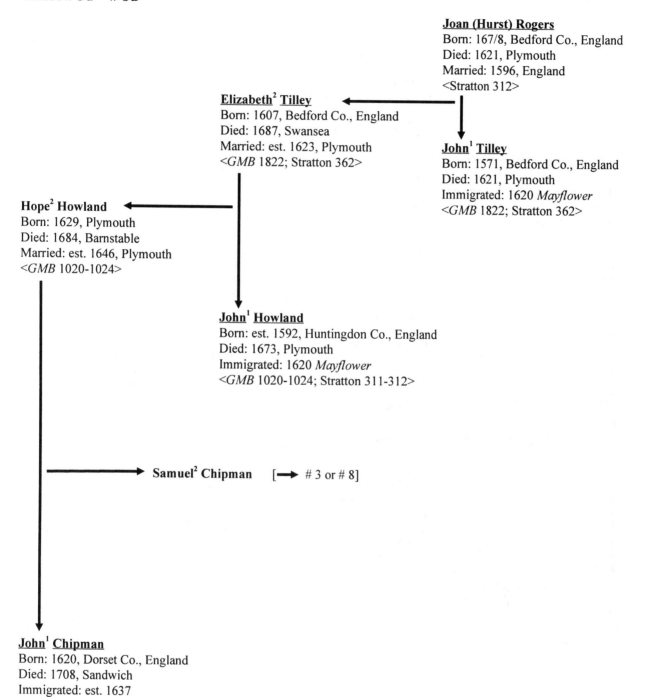

Joan (Hurst) Rogers
Born: 167/8, Bedford Co., England
Died: 1621, Plymouth
Married: 1596, England
<Stratton 312>

Elizabeth² Tilley
Born: 1607, Bedford Co., England
Died: 1687, Swansea
Married: est. 1623, Plymouth
<*GMB* 1822; Stratton 362>

John¹ Tilley
Born: 1571, Bedford Co., England
Died: 1621, Plymouth
Immigrated: 1620 *Mayflower*
<*GMB* 1822; Stratton 362>

Hope² Howland
Born: 1629, Plymouth
Died: 1684, Barnstable
Married: est. 1646, Plymouth
<*GMB* 1020-1024>

John¹ Howland
Born: est. 1592, Huntingdon Co., England
Died: 1673, Plymouth
Immigrated: 1620 *Mayflower*
<*GMB* 1020-1024; Stratton 311-312>

Samuel² Chipman   [⟶ # 3 or # 8]

John¹ Chipman
Born: 1620, Dorset Co., England
Died: 1708, Sandwich
Immigrated: est. 1637
<Chipman #1; Stratton 262-263>

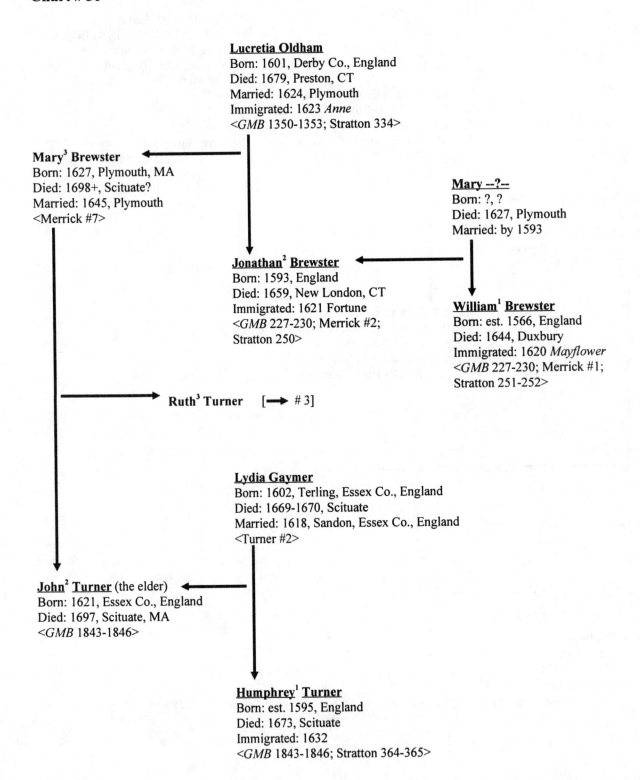

Lucretia Oldham
Born: 1601, Derby Co., England
Died: 1679, Preston, CT
Married: 1624, Plymouth
Immigrated: 1623 *Anne*
<*GMB* 1350-1353; Stratton 334>

Mary³ Brewster
Born: 1627, Plymouth, MA
Died: 1698+, Scituate?
Married: 1645, Plymouth
<Merrick #7>

Mary --?--
Born: ?, ?
Died: 1627, Plymouth
Married: by 1593

Jonathan² Brewster
Born: 1593, England
Died: 1659, New London, CT
Immigrated: 1621 Fortune
<*GMB* 227-230; Merrick #2;
Stratton 250>

William¹ Brewster
Born: est. 1566, England
Died: 1644, Duxbury
Immigrated: 1620 *Mayflower*
<*GMB* 227-230; Merrick #1;
Stratton 251-252>

Ruth³ Turner   [⟶ # 3]

Lydia Gaymer
Born: 1602, Terling, Essex Co., England
Died: 1669-1670, Scituate
Married: 1618, Sandon, Essex Co., England
<Turner #2>

John² Turner (the elder)
Born: 1621, Essex Co., England
Died: 1697, Scituate, MA
<*GMB* 1843-1846>

Humphrey¹ Turner
Born: est. 1595, England
Died: 1673, Scituate
Immigrated: 1632
<*GMB* 1843-1846; Stratton 364-365>

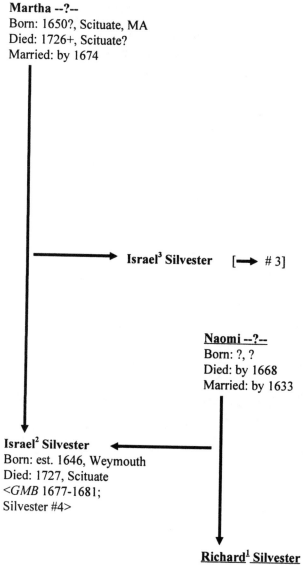

Martha --?--
Born: 1650?, Scituate, MA
Died: 1726+, Scituate?
Married: by 1674

Israel³ Silvester [→ # 3]

Naomi --?--
Born: ?, ?
Died: by 1668
Married: by 1633

Israel² Silvester
Born: est. 1646, Weymouth
Died: 1727, Scituate
<*GMB* 1677-1681;
Silvester #4>

Richard¹ Silvester
Born: est. 1608, England
Died: 1663, Marshfield
Immigrated: 1630
<*GMB* 1677-1681; Stratton 352-353; Silvester #1>

117

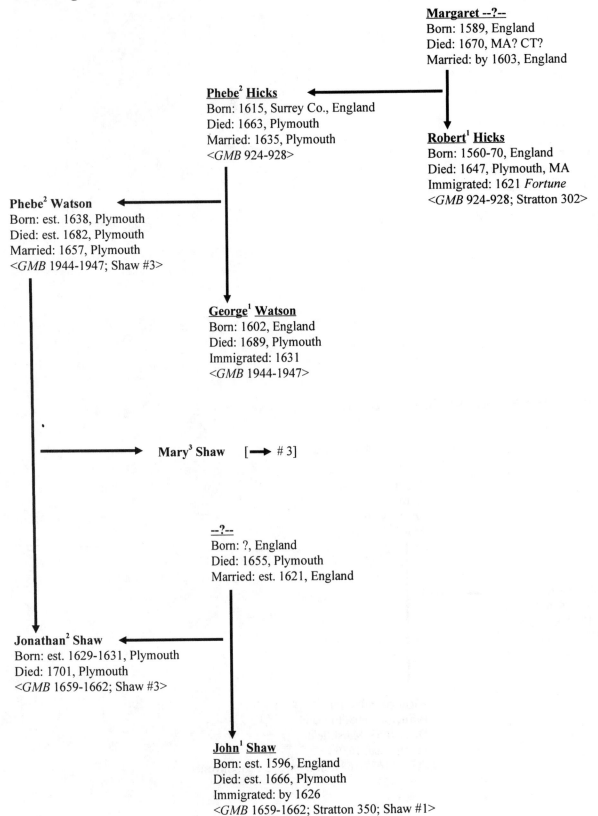

Margaret --?--
Born: 1589, England
Died: 1670, MA? CT?
Married: by 1603, England

Phebe² Hicks
Born: 1615, Surrey Co., England
Died: 1663, Plymouth
Married: 1635, Plymouth
<GMB 924-928>

Robert¹ Hicks
Born: 1560-70, England
Died: 1647, Plymouth, MA
Immigrated: 1621 *Fortune*
<GMB 924-928; Stratton 302>

Phebe² Watson
Born: est. 1638, Plymouth
Died: est. 1682, Plymouth
Married: 1657, Plymouth
<GMB 1944-1947; Shaw #3>

George¹ Watson
Born: 1602, England
Died: 1689, Plymouth
Immigrated: 1631
<GMB 1944-1947>

Mary³ Shaw   [⟶ # 3]

--?--
Born: ?, England
Died: 1655, Plymouth
Married: est. 1621, England

Jonathan² Shaw
Born: est. 1629-1631, Plymouth
Died: 1701, Plymouth
<GMB 1659-1662; Shaw #3>

John¹ Shaw
Born: est. 1596, England
Died: est. 1666, Plymouth
Immigrated: by 1626
<GMB 1659-1662; Stratton 350; Shaw #1>

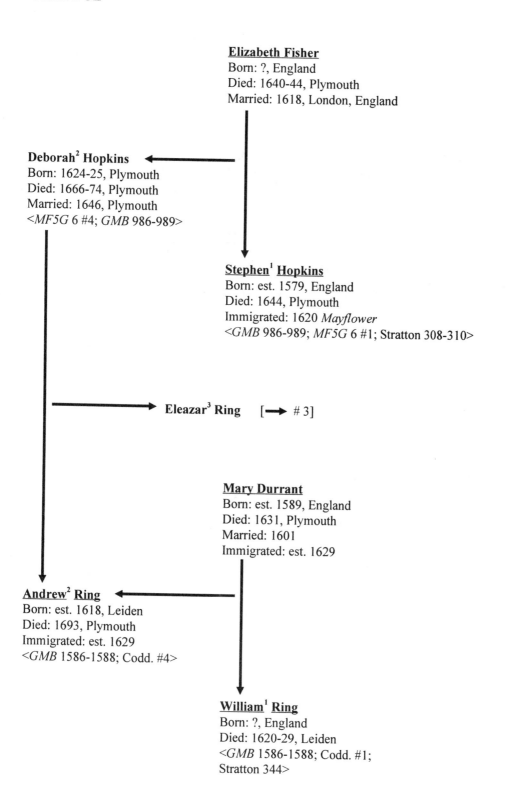

Elizabeth Fisher
Born: ?, England
Died: 1640-44, Plymouth
Married: 1618, London, England

Deborah² Hopkins
Born: 1624-25, Plymouth
Died: 1666-74, Plymouth
Married: 1646, Plymouth
<*MF5G* 6 #4; *GMB* 986-989>

Stephen¹ Hopkins
Born: est. 1579, England
Died: 1644, Plymouth
Immigrated: 1620 *Mayflower*
<*GMB* 986-989; *MF5G* 6 #1; Stratton 308-310>

Eleazar³ Ring   [➝ # 3]

Mary Durrant
Born: est. 1589, England
Died: 1631, Plymouth
Married: 1601
Immigrated: est. 1629

Andrew² Ring
Born: est. 1618, Leiden
Died: 1693, Plymouth
Immigrated: est. 1629
<*GMB* 1586-1588; Codd. #4>

William¹ Ring
Born: ?, England
Died: 1620-29, Leiden
<*GMB* 1586-1588; Codd. #1;
Stratton 344>

Charts 4, 4a-4c, 4e, and 4g-4h

Ancestry of Ephraim[5] Cook
(1737-1821)
of
Plymouth County, Massachusetts,
and
Yarmouth County, Nova Scotia

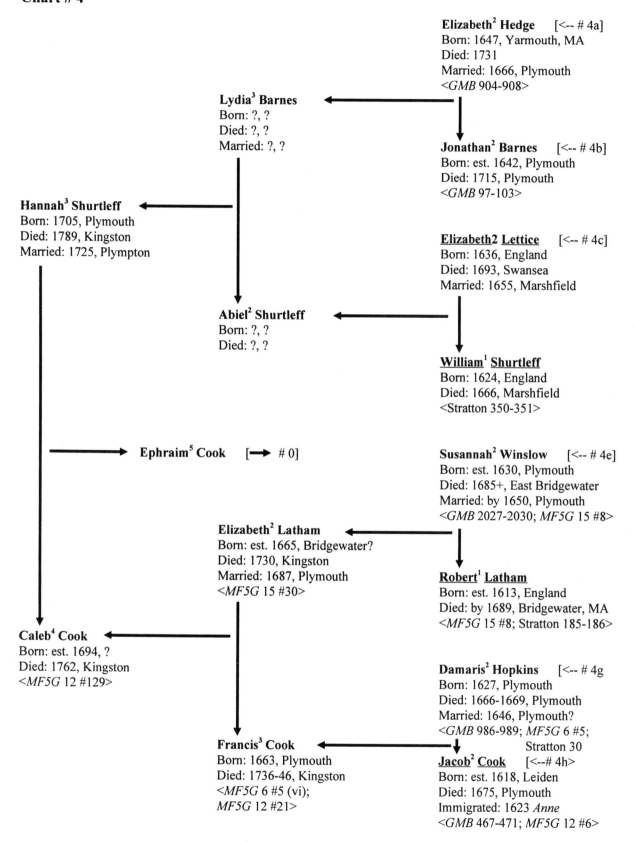

Elizabeth² Hedge   [<-- # 4a]
Born: 1647, Yarmouth, MA
Died: 1731
Married: 1666, Plymouth
<GMB 904-908>

Lydia³ Barnes
Born: ?, ?
Died: ?, ?
Married: ?, ?

Jonathan² Barnes   [<-- # 4b]
Born: est. 1642, Plymouth
Died: 1715, Plymouth
<GMB 97-103>

Hannah³ Shurtleff
Born: 1705, Plymouth
Died: 1789, Kingston
Married: 1725, Plympton

Elizabeth2 Lettice   [<-- # 4c]
Born: 1636, England
Died: 1693, Swansea
Married: 1655, Marshfield

Abiel² Shurtleff
Born: ?, ?
Died: ?, ?

William¹ Shurtleff
Born: 1624, England
Died: 1666, Marshfield
<Stratton 350-351>

Ephraim⁵ Cook   [➞ # 0]

Susannah² Winslow   [<-- # 4e]
Born: est. 1630, Plymouth
Died: 1685+, East Bridgewater
Married: by 1650, Plymouth
<GMB 2027-2030; MF5G 15 #8>

Elizabeth² Latham
Born: est. 1665, Bridgewater?
Died: 1730, Kingston
Married: 1687, Plymouth
<MF5G 15 #30>

Robert¹ Latham
Born: est. 1613, England
Died: by 1689, Bridgewater, MA
<MF5G 15 #8; Stratton 185-186>

Caleb⁴ Cook
Born: est. 1694, ?
Died: 1762, Kingston
<MF5G 12 #129>

Damaris² Hopkins   [<-- # 4g
Born: 1627, Plymouth
Died: 1666-1669, Plymouth
Married: 1646, Plymouth?
<GMB 986-989; MF5G 6 #5;
                          Stratton 30

Francis³ Cook
Born: 1663, Plymouth
Died: 1736-46, Kingston
<MF5G 6 #5 (vi);
MF5G 12 #21>

Jacob² Cook   [<--# 4h]
Born: est. 1618, Leiden
Died: 1675, Plymouth
Immigrated: 1623 *Anne*
<GMB 467-471; MF5G 12 #6>

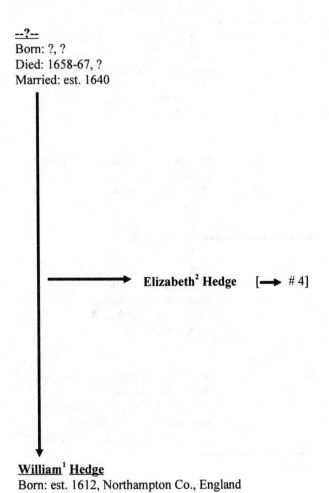

--?--
Born: ?, ?
Died: 1658-67, ?
Married: est. 1640

Elizabeth[2] Hedge   [⟶ # 4]

William[1] Hedge
Born: est. 1612, Northampton Co., England
Died: 1670, Yarmouth, MA
Immigrated: 1633
<*GMB* 904-908; Stratton 300-301>

Ancestry of Adriana Porter
Chart # 4b

<u>**Mary Plummer**</u>
Born: ?, England
Died: 1651, Plymouth
Married: 1633, Plymouth
<Stratton 339>

→ **Jonathan[2] Barnes** [→ # 4]

<u>**John[1] Barnes**</u>
Born: est. 1608, England
Died 1668-71, Plymouth
Immigrated: 1632
<*GMB* 97-103; Stratton 240-241>

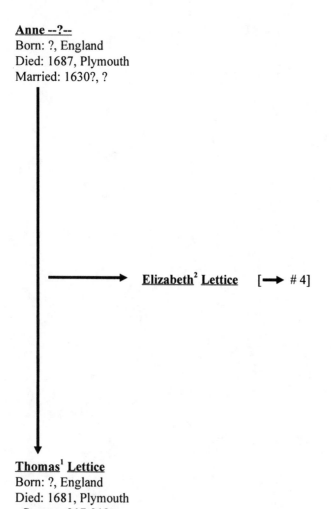

Anne --?--
Born: ?, England
Died: 1687, Plymouth
Married: 1630?, ?

Elizabeth² Lettice   [→ # 4]

Thomas¹ Lettice
Born: ?, England
Died: 1681, Plymouth
<Stratton 317-318>

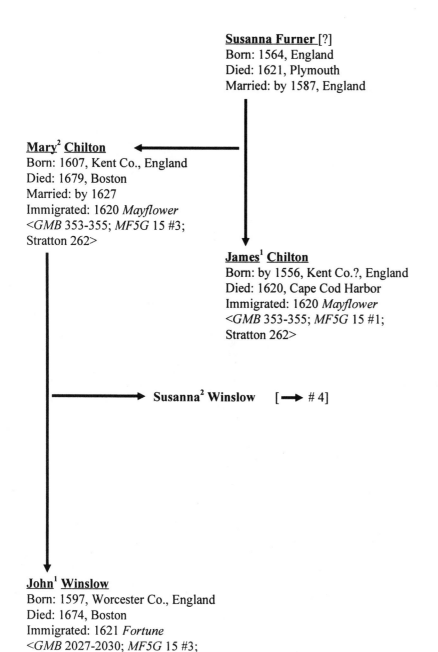

Susanna Furner [?]
Born: 1564, England
Died: 1621, Plymouth
Married: by 1587, England

Mary² Chilton
Born: 1607, Kent Co., England
Died: 1679, Boston
Married: by 1627
Immigrated: 1620 *Mayflower*
<*GMB* 353-355; *MF5G* 15 #3;
Stratton 262>

James¹ Chilton
Born: by 1556, Kent Co.?, England
Died: 1620, Cape Cod Harbor
Immigrated: 1620 *Mayflower*
<*GMB* 353-355; *MF5G* 15 #1;
Stratton 262>

Susanna² Winslow   [➔ # 4]

John¹ Winslow
Born: 1597, Worcester Co., England
Died: 1674, Boston
Immigrated: 1621 *Fortune*
<*GMB* 2027-2030; *MF5G* 15 #3;
Stratton 374-375>

Ancestry of Adriana Porter
Chart # 4g

<u>**Elizabeth Fisher**</u>
Born: ?, England
Died: 1640-44, Plymouth
Married: 1618, London, England

→ **Damaris[2] Hopkins** [→ # 4]

<u>**Stephen[1] Hopkins**</u>
Born: est. 1579, England
Died: 1644, Plymouth
Immigrated: 1620 *Mayflower*
<*GMB* 986-989; *MF5G* 6 #1;
Stratton 308-310>

Hester Mahieu
Born: 1582-88?, Kent Co., England?
Died: 1666+, Plymouth
Married: 1603, Leiden
Immigrated: 1623 *Anne*

Jacob² Cook   [→ # 4]

Francis¹ Cook
Born: est. 1583, England
Died: 1663, Plymouth
Immigrated: 1620 *Mayflower*
<*GMB* 467-471; *MF5G* 12 #1;
Stratton 270>

Chart 7

Ancestry of Mary[2] Tardy
(1760-1836)
of
Essex County, Massachusetts,
and
Yarmouth County, Nova Scotia

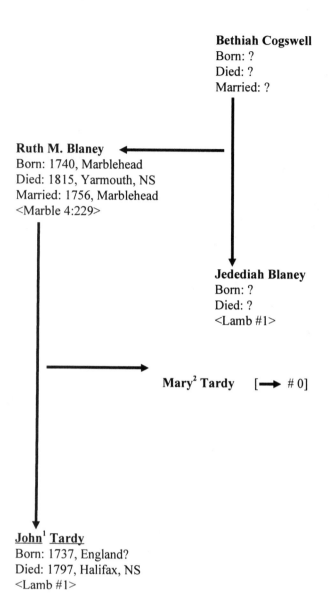

Bethiah Cogswell
Born: ?
Died: ?
Married: ?

Ruth M. Blaney ◄─────────
Born: 1740, Marblehead
Died: 1815, Yarmouth, NS
Married: 1756, Marblehead
<Marble 4:229>

Jedediah Blaney
Born: ?
Died: ?
<Lamb #1>

Mary² Tardy   [──► # 0]

John¹ Tardy
Born: 1737, England?
Died: 1797, Halifax, NS
<Lamb #1>

*Note: The information in Chart #7 became available just weeks before this book went to press. There has not been time to trace the ancestry of Ruth M. Blaney further, though it could doubtless be carried back to her first immigrant ancestors, three or four generations before her, without much additional work. It seems likely that John Tardy was born in England, and thus was himself the first immigrant ancestor in his line.

Charts 8 and 8a - 8h

Ancestry of Nehemiah[6] Porter
(1753-1806+)
of
Essex County, Massachusetts,
and
Yarmouth County, Nova Scotia

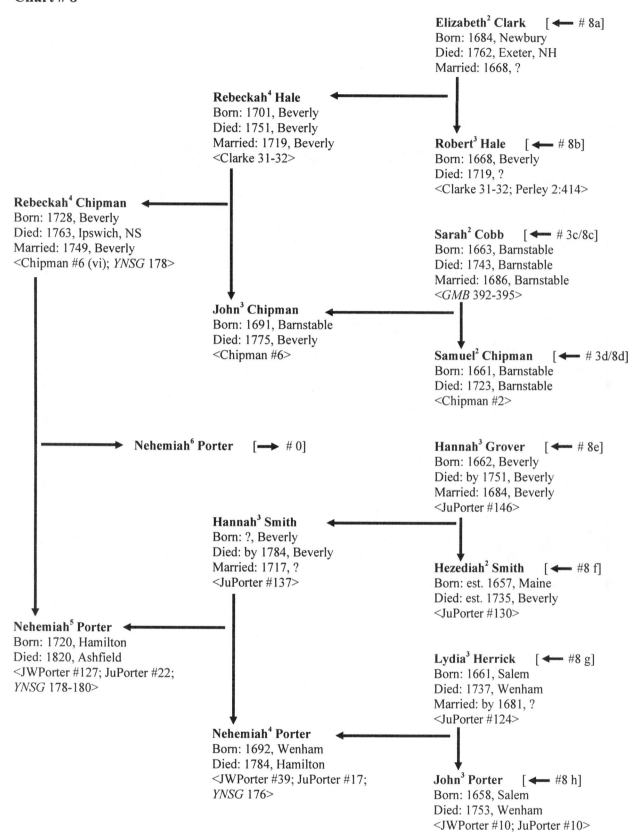

Elizabeth² Clark [← # 8a]
Born: 1684, Newbury
Died: 1762, Exeter, NH
Married: 1668, ?

Rebeckah⁴ Hale
Born: 1701, Beverly
Died: 1751, Beverly
Married: 1719, Beverly
<Clarke 31-32>

Robert³ Hale [← # 8b]
Born: 1668, Beverly
Died: 1719, ?
<Clarke 31-32; Perley 2:414>

Rebeckah⁴ Chipman
Born: 1728, Beverly
Died: 1763, Ipswich, NS
Married: 1749, Beverly
<Chipman #6 (vi); *YNSG* 178>

Sarah² Cobb [← # 3c/8c]
Born: 1663, Barnstable
Died: 1743, Barnstable
Married: 1686, Barnstable
<*GMB* 392-395>

John³ Chipman
Born: 1691, Barnstable
Died: 1775, Beverly
<Chipman #6>

Samuel² Chipman [← # 3d/8d]
Born: 1661, Barnstable
Died: 1723, Barnstable
<Chipman #2>

Nehemiah⁶ Porter [→ # 0]

Hannah³ Grover [← # 8e]
Born: 1662, Beverly
Died: by 1751, Beverly
Married: 1684, Beverly
<JuPorter #146>

Hannah³ Smith
Born: ?, Beverly
Died: by 1784, Beverly
Married: 1717, ?
<JuPorter #137>

Hezediah² Smith [← #8 f]
Born: est. 1657, Maine
Died: est. 1735, Beverly
<JuPorter #130>

Nehemiah⁵ Porter
Born: 1720, Hamilton
Died: 1820, Ashfield
<JWPorter #127; JuPorter #22;
YNSG 178-180>

Lydia³ Herrick [← #8 g]
Born: 1661, Salem
Died: 1737, Wenham
Married: by 1681, ?
<JuPorter #124>

Nehemiah⁴ Porter
Born: 1692, Wenham
Died: 1784, Hamilton
<JWPorter #39; JuPorter #17;
YNSG 176>

John³ Porter [← #8 h]
Born: 1658, Salem
Died: 1753, Wenham
<JWPorter #10; JuPorter #10>

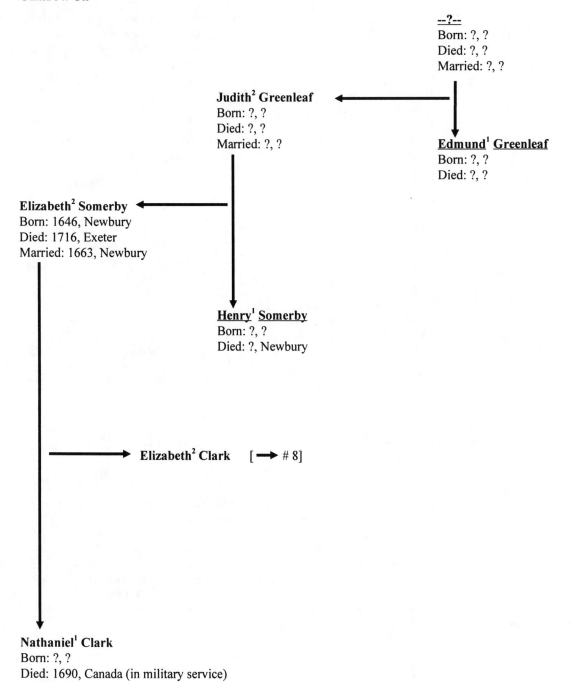

--?--
Born: ?, ?
Died: ?, ?
Married: ?, ?

Judith² Greenleaf
Born: ?, ?
Died: ?, ?
Married: ?, ?

Edmund¹ Greenleaf
Born: ?, ?
Died: ?, ?

Elizabeth² Somerby
Born: 1646, Newbury
Died: 1716, Exeter
Married: 1663, Newbury

Henry¹ Somerby
Born: ?, ?
Died: ?, Newbury

Elizabeth² Clark   [➝ # 8]

Nathaniel¹ Clark
Born: ?, ?
Died: 1690, Canada (in military service)
<Clarke 9-39>

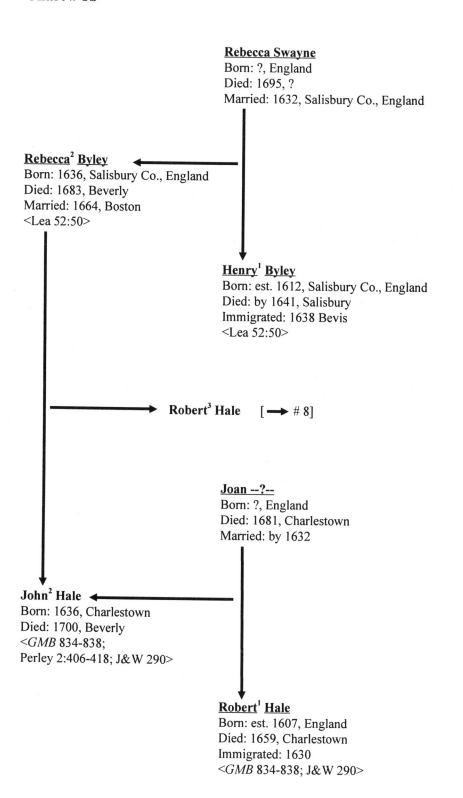

Rebecca Swayne
Born: ?, England
Died: 1695, ?
Married: 1632, Salisbury Co., England

Rebecca² Byley
Born: 1636, Salisbury Co., England
Died: 1683, Beverly
Married: 1664, Boston
<Lea 52:50>

Henry¹ Byley
Born: est. 1612, Salisbury Co., England
Died: by 1641, Salisbury
Immigrated: 1638 Bevis
<Lea 52:50>

Robert³ Hale   [⟶ # 8]

Joan --?--
Born: ?, England
Died: 1681, Charlestown
Married: by 1632

John² Hale
Born: 1636, Charlestown
Died: 1700, Beverly
<*GMB* 834-838;
Perley 2:406-418; J&W 290>

Robert¹ Hale
Born: est. 1607, England
Died: 1659, Charlestown
Immigrated: 1630
<*GMB* 834-838; J&W 290>

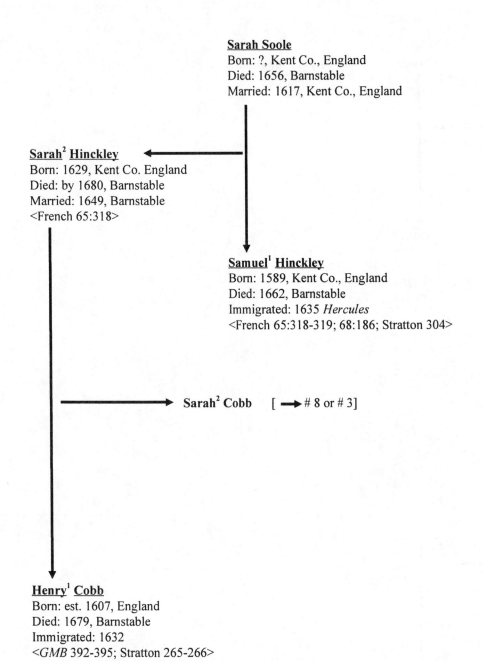

Sarah Soole
Born: ?, Kent Co., England
Died: 1656, Barnstable
Married: 1617, Kent Co., England

Sarah² Hinckley
Born: 1629, Kent Co. England
Died: by 1680, Barnstable
Married: 1649, Barnstable
<French 65:318>

Samuel¹ Hinckley
Born: 1589, Kent Co., England
Died: 1662, Barnstable
Immigrated: 1635 *Hercules*
<French 65:318-319; 68:186; Stratton 304>

Sarah² Cobb   [⟶ # 8 or # 3]

Henry¹ Cobb
Born: est. 1607, England
Died: 1679, Barnstable
Immigrated: 1632
<*GMB* 392-395; Stratton 265-266>

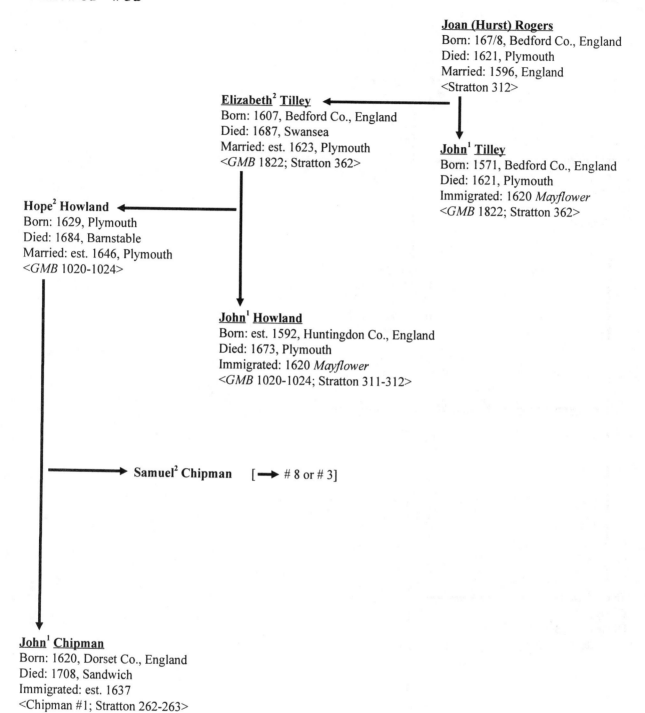

Joan (Hurst) Rogers
Born: 167/8, Bedford Co., England
Died: 1621, Plymouth
Married: 1596, England
<Stratton 312>

Elizabeth² Tilley
Born: 1607, Bedford Co., England
Died: 1687, Swansea
Married: est. 1623, Plymouth
<*GMB* 1822; Stratton 362>

John¹ Tilley
Born: 1571, Bedford Co., England
Died: 1621, Plymouth
Immigrated: 1620 *Mayflower*
<*GMB* 1822; Stratton 362>

Hope² Howland
Born: 1629, Plymouth
Died: 1684, Barnstable
Married: est. 1646, Plymouth
<*GMB* 1020-1024>

John¹ Howland
Born: est. 1592, Huntingdon Co., England
Died: 1673, Plymouth
Immigrated: 1620 *Mayflower*
<*GMB* 1020-1024; Stratton 311-312>

Samuel² Chipman   [➔ # 8 or # 3]

John¹ Chipman
Born: 1620, Dorset Co., England
Died: 1708, Sandwich
Immigrated: est. 1637
<Chipman #1; Stratton 262-263>

Ancestry of Adriana Porter
Chart # 8e

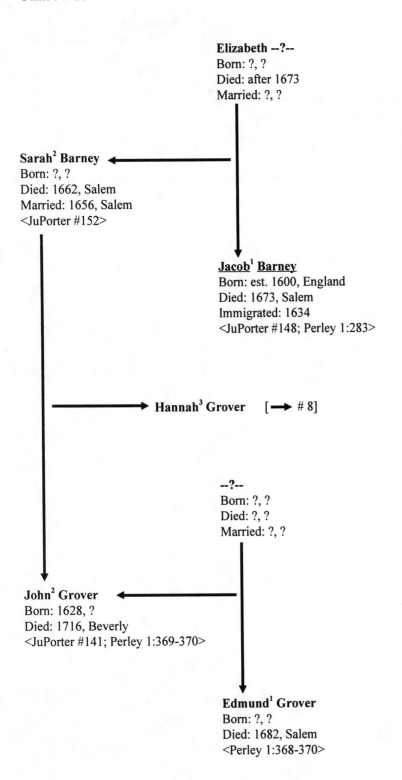

Elizabeth --?--
Born: ?, ?
Died: after 1673
Married: ?, ?

Sarah² Barney
Born: ?, ?
Died: 1662, Salem
Married: 1656, Salem
<JuPorter #152>

Jacob¹ Barney
Born: est. 1600, England
Died: 1673, Salem
Immigrated: 1634
<JuPorter #148; Perley 1:283>

Hannah³ Grover   [→ # 8]

--?--
Born: ?, ?
Died: ?, ?
Married: ?, ?

John² Grover
Born: 1628, ?
Died: 1716, Beverly
<JuPorter #141; Perley 1:369-370>

Edmund¹ Grover
Born: ?, ?
Died: 1682, Salem
<Perley 1:368-370>

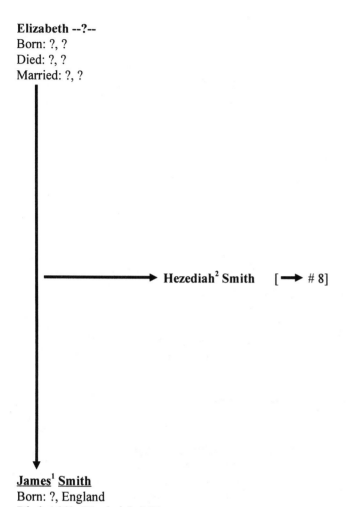

Elizabeth --?--
Born: ?, ?
Died: ?, ?
Married: ?, ?

Hezediah[2] Smith   [➔ # 8]

James[1] Smith
Born: ?, England
Died: 1660, Woolwich, ME
<JuPorter #129>

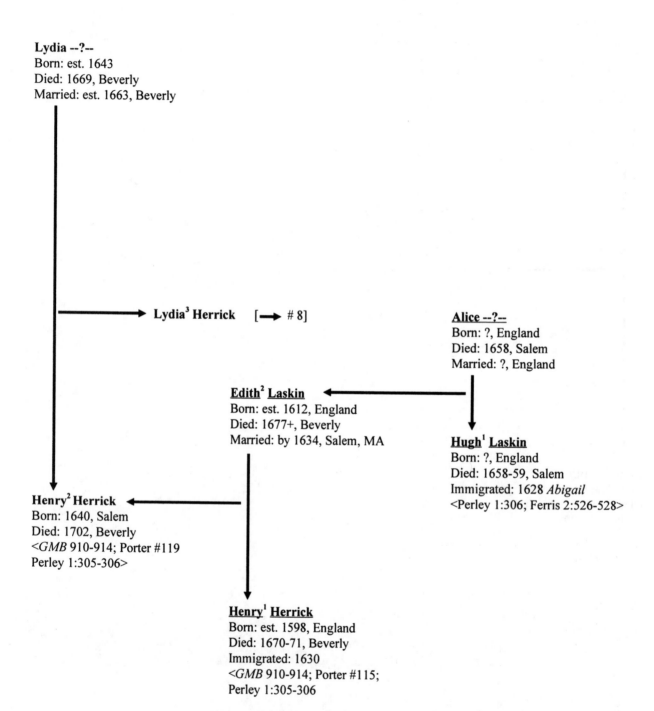

Lydia --?--
Born: est. 1643
Died: 1669, Beverly
Married: est. 1663, Beverly

Lydia[3] Herrick   [→ # 8]

Alice --?--
Born: ?, England
Died: 1658, Salem
Married: ?, England

Edith[2] Laskin
Born: est. 1612, England
Died: 1677+, Beverly
Married: by 1634, Salem, MA

Hugh[1] Laskin
Born: ?, England
Died: 1658-59, Salem
Immigrated: 1628 *Abigail*
<Perley 1:306; Ferris 2:526-528>

Henry[2] Herrick
Born: 1640, Salem
Died: 1702, Beverly
<*GMB* 910-914; Porter #119
Perley 1:305-306>

Henry[1] Herrick
Born: est. 1598, England
Died: 1670-71, Beverly
Immigrated: 1630
<*GMB* 910-914; Porter #115;
Perley 1:305-306

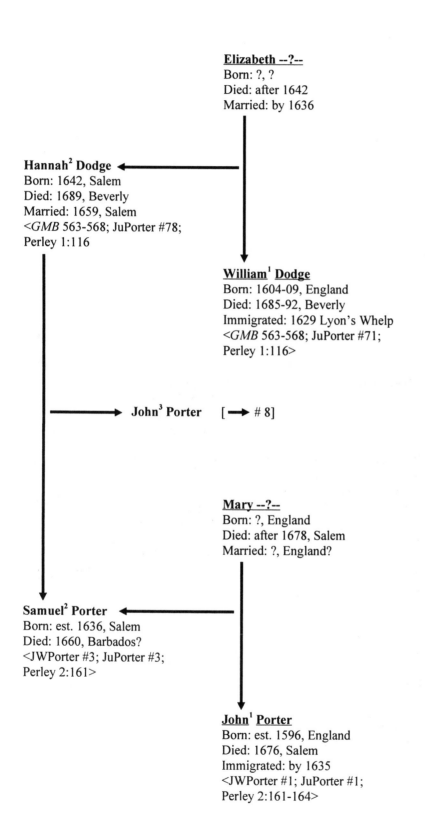

Elizabeth --?--
Born: ?, ?
Died: after 1642
Married: by 1636

Hannah² Dodge
Born: 1642, Salem
Died: 1689, Beverly
Married: 1659, Salem
<*GMB* 563-568; JuPorter #78;
Perley 1:116

William¹ Dodge
Born: 1604-09, England
Died: 1685-92, Beverly
Immigrated: 1629 Lyon's Whelp
<*GMB* 563-568; JuPorter #71;
Perley 1:116>

John³ Porter   [⟶ # 8]

Mary --?--
Born: ?, England
Died: after 1678, Salem
Married: ?, England?

Samuel² Porter
Born: est. 1636, Salem
Died: 1660, Barbados?
<JWPorter #3; JuPorter #3;
Perley 2:161>

John¹ Porter
Born: est. 1596, England
Died: 1676, Salem
Immigrated: by 1635
<JWPorter #1; JuPorter #1;
Perley 2:161-164>

Appendix B
Works Cited in the Charts

**Abbreviations
Used in
Charts**

Chipman   Chipman, John Hale III. *A Chipman Genealogy.* Norwell, Mass:
                   Chipman Historics, 1970.

Clarke   Clarke, George Kuhn. *The Descendants of Nathaniel Clarke and
                   his Wife, Elizabeth Somerby, of Newbury, Massachusetts: A
                   History of Ten Generations, 1642-1902.* Special ed. Boston:
                   Self-published, 1902.

Codd.   Coddington, John Insley. "The Widow Mary Ring, of Plymouth,
                   Massachusetts, and her Children." *The American Genealogist*
                   42 (1966): 193-205.

Ferris   Ferris, Mary Walton. *Dawes-Gates Ancestral Lines,* vol. 1.
                   Milwaukee: Self-published (The Wisconsin Cuneo Press), 1943;
                   vol. 2. Chicago: Self-published (The Lakeside Press), 1931.

French   French, Elizabeth. "Genealogical Research in England."
                   [Hinckley, Soole.] The *NEHGR* 65 (1911): 287-90, 314-319;
                   68 (1914): 186-89; 75 (1921): 238.
                   [Hatch.] The *NEHGR* 70 (1916): 245-60.

GGTrask   Trask, Gwen Guiou. *Elias Trask, his Children, and their
                   Succeeding Race: The Trasks of Nova Scotia.* Yarmouth, N.S.:
                   Sentinal Printing Ltd., 1979. *Elias Trask, his Children and their
                   Succeeding Race: The Trasks of Nova Scotia,* 2nd ed.
                   Yarmouth, N.S.: Stoneycroft Publishing, 2002.

GMB   Anderson, Robert Charles. *The Great Migration Begins:
                   Immigrants to New England, 1620-1633,* 3 vols. Boston:
                   The New England Historic Genealogical Society, 1995.
                   Revised ed., 2000. [Ancestry View CD]

Abbreviations Used in Charts

Holman	Holman, Mary Lovering. *Descendants of William Sherman of Marshfield, Massachusetts.* Concord, N.H.: Self-published (Rumford Press): 1936.
J&W	Jacobus, Donald Lines and Edgar Francis Waterman. *Hale, House, and Related Families, Mainly of the Connecticut River Valley.* Hartford: The Connecticut Historical Society, 1952.
JuPorter	Porter, Juliette. *A Porter Pedigree, Being an Account of the Ancestry and Descendants of Samuel and Martha (Perley) Porter of Chester, New Hampshire, Who were Descendants of John Porter of Salem, Massachusetts and of Allan Perley of Ipswich, Massachusetts.* Worcester, Mass.: Self-published, 1907.
JWPorter	Porter, Joseph W. *A Genealogy of the Descendants of Richard Porter, who Settled at Weymouth, Massachusetts, 1635, and Allied Families: Also, Some Account of the Descendants of John Porter, who Settled at Hingham, Massachusetts, 1635, and Salem (Danvers), Massachusetts, 1644.* Bangor, Me.: Self-published (Burr and Robinson), 1878.
Lamb	Lamb, Kathleen P. *Capt. John Tardy and His Family.* Self-published, Rockwood, Tenn., 1999.
Lea	Lea, J. Henry. "The English Ancestry of the Families of Batt and Byley of Salisbury, Mass." The *NEHGR* 51 (1897): 181-88, 348-57; 52 (1898): 44-51, 321-22.
Marble	Marble, Allan Everett. *Deaths, Burials, and Probate of Nova Scotians, 1800-1850, from Primary Sources,* 4 vols. Genealogical Association of Nova Scotia, Publications #22-25. Halifax, N.S., 1999.

Abbreviations Used in Charts

Merrick   Merrick, Barbara Lambert. *William Brewster of the Mayflower and his Descendants for Four Generations,* 3rd ed. (Mayflower Families in Progress.) Plymouth: General Society of *Mayflower* Descendants, 2000.
[continued by]
Merrick, Barbara Lambert. *William Brewster of the Mayflower and the Fifth Generation Descendants of his Son Jonathan.*[2] (Mayflower Families in Progress.) Plymouth: General Society of *Mayflower* Descendants, 1999.

MF5G   *Mayflower Families Through Five Generations.* Edited by Robert S. Wakefield, et al. Plymouth: General Society of *Mayflower* Descendants, 1975-present.
[Cited here by volume and entry number.]
Vol. 5, *Edward Winslow; John Billington,* 1991. [Citations are to Billington lines.]
Vol. 6, *Stephen Hopkins,* 1992, 2nd ed., 1995.
Vol. 9, *Francis Eaton,* rev. ed., 1996.
Vol. 10, *Samuel Fuller,* rev. ed., 1996.
Vol. 12, *Francis Cooke,* 1996.
Vol. 15, *James Chilton; Richard More,* rev. ed., 1997. [Citations are to Chilton lines.]
Vol. 16, *John Alden,* Part 1, 1999.

NEHGR   The *New England Historical and Genealogical Register,* 154 vols. to date. Boston: The New England Historic Genealogical Society, 1847ff.

Perley   Perley, Sidney. *The History of Salem, Massachusetts,* 3 vols. Salem: Sidney Perley, 1924-1928.

Putnam   Putnam, Eben. *A History of the Putnam Family in England and America.* Salem: The Salem Press, 1891.

Shaw   Shaw, Jonathan A. "John Shaw of Plymouth Colony, Purchaser and Canal Builder." The *NEHGR* 151 (1997): 259-85, 417-38.

Abbreviations Used in Charts

Silvester — Silvester, Albert Henry. "Richard Silvester of Weymouth, Massachusetts, and Some of his Descendants." *NEHGR* 85 (1931): 247-65, 357-71; 86 (1932): 84-93, 120-32, 286-99; 87 (1933): 84.

Stratton — Stratton, Eugene Aubrey. *Plymouth Colony, its History and People, 1620-1691.* Salt Lake City: Ancestry Publishing, 1986.

Turner — Turner, Vernon Dow. "Lydia Gaymer, the Wife of Humphrey Turner of Scituate." *NEHGR* 151 (1997): 286-90.

WBTrask — Trask, William Blake. [Cited by volume and page, e.g., 55:321.] "Captain William Traske of Salem, Massachusetts." *NEHGR* 53 (1899), 43-53 and 2 plates.
"The Traske Family in England." *NEHGR* 54 (1900), 279-83.
"Captain William Traske and Some of his Descendants." *NEHGR* 55 (1901), 321-30 and 1 plate, 385-88; 56 (1902), 69-73; 199-202; 397-401; 57 (1903), 65-67; 384-86.

YNSG — Brown, George S. *Yarmouth, Nova Scotia, Genealogies, Transcribed form the Yarmouth Herald.* Prepared for publishing by Martha and William Reamy. Baltimore: Genealogical Publishing Co., 1993. [Also available as Brøderbund CD #274.]

Appendix C
Index of Persons in the Charts

Name	Chart Number
Alden: John[1] > Joseph[2] > Joseph[3] > Mehitable[4]	1 < 1b
Ballou: Abigail	1a
Barnes: John1 > Jonathan[2] > Lydia[3]	4 < 4b
Billington: John[1](+Eleanor -?-) > Francis[2] > Martha[3]	1d
Blaney: Jedediah > Ruth	7
Brewster: William[1](+Mary -?-) > Jonathan[2] > Mary[3]	3e
Byley: Henry[1](+Rebecca -?-) > Rebecca[2]	8b
Chilton: James[1] > Mary[2]	4e
Chipman: John[1] > Samuel[2] > John[3] > Rebecca[4]	8 < 3d/8d
Chipman: John[1] > Samuel[2] > Jacob[3] > Lucy[4]	3 < 3d/8d
Clark: Nathaniel[1] > Elizabeth[2]	8 < 8a
Clements (Clemons): Samuel1 > John[2] > John[3] > Mehitable[4]	0 < 1
Cobb: Henry[1] > Sarah[2]	3 or 8 < 3c/8c
Coggswell: Bethiah	7
Cook: Francis[1] > Jacob[2] > Francis[3] > Caleb[4] > Ephraim[5] > John[6] > Sarah Arnot[7]	0 < 4 < 4h
Dodge: William[1](+Elizabeth -?-) > Hannah2	8h
Dunham: John[1] > Daniel[2] > Hannah[3]	1 < 1a
Durrant: Mary	3h
Eaton: Francis[1](+Sarah -?-) > Samuel[2] > Samuel[3] > Barnabas[4] > Hannah[5]	1 < 1d
Fisher: Elizabeth	3h or 4g
Fuller: Samuel[1] > Samuel[2] > Elizabeth[3]	1 < 1c
Furner [?]: Susanna	4e
Gaymer: Lydia	3e
Greenleaf: Edmund[1](+-?-) > Judith[2]	8a
Greenwood: Martha	0
Grover: ?[1] > Hannah[2]	8 < 8e
Hale: Robert[1](+Joan -?-) > John[2] > Robert[3] > Rebecca[4]	8 < 8b
Hatch: William[1] > Walter[2] > Jane[3]	8a
Hayward: Thomas[1](+Martha -?-) > Mehitable[2]	1a
Hedge: William[1](+-?-) > Elizabeth[2]	4 < 4a
Henderson: Mary	1
Herrick: Henry[1] > Henry[2](+Lydia -?-) > Lydia[3]	8 < 8g
Hicks: Robert[1](+Margaret -?-) > Phebe[2]	3g
Hill: Prudence	8a
Hinckley: Samuel[1] > Sarah[2]	3c/8c
Holbrooke: Thomas[1](+Jane -?-) > Elizabeth[2]	3a
Holyoke: Edward[1] > Ann[2]	2g
Hopkins: Stephen[1] > Deborah[2]	3h

Hopkins: Stephen[1] > Damaris[2]   4 < 4g
Howland: John[1] > Hope[2]   3d/8d
Hurst: Joan   3d/8d

Laskin: Hugh[1](+Alice -?-) > Edith[2]   8g
Latham: Robert[1] > Elizabeth[2]   4
Lee: Bridget   1c
Lettice: Thomas[1](+Anne -?-) > Elizabeth[2]   4 + 4c

Mahieu: Hester   4h
Mullins: William[1](+Alice -?-) > Priscilla[2]   1b

Nichols: John[1](+-?-)> Elizabeth[2]   1c

Oldham: Lucretia   3e

Penn: Christian   1d
Phillips: Alice   3g
Pitney: James[1] > Sarah[2]   3b
Plummer: Mary   4b
Porter: John[1](+Mary -?-) > Samuel2 > John[3] > Nehemiah[4] > Nehemiah[5]
   > Nehemiah[6] > John Tardy[7] > Henry[8] > Adriana[9]   8 < 8h
Putnam: John[1](+Priscilla -?-) > Thomas[2] > Ann[3]   2 < 2g

Ring: William[1] > Andrew[2] > Eleazar[3] > Samuel[4] > George[5] > Louisa[6]   0 < 3 < 3h
Rogers: Lydia   2

Shaw: John[1] > Jonathan[2] > Mary[3]   3 < 3g
Sherman: William[1] > John[2] > Bethiah[3]   3 < 3a
Shurtleff: William[1] > Abiel[2] > Hannah[3]   4
Silvester: Richard1(+Naomi -?-) > Israel[2](+Martha -?-) > Israel[3] > Ruth[4]   3 < 3f
Simonson: Moses1(+Sarah -?-) > Mary[2]   1b
Smith: ?[1] > Hezediah[2] > Hannah[3]   8 < 8f
Smith: Sarah   3b
Somerby: Henry[1] > Elizabeth[2]   8a
Soole: Sarah   3c/8c
Stockton: Prudence   2g

Tardy: John[1] > Mary[2]   0 < 7
Thomas: John[1] > Israel[2] > Bethiah[3]   3 < 3b
Tilley: John[1] > Elizabeth[2]   3d/8d
Trask: William[1](+Sarah -?-) > William[2] > William[3] > Elias[4] > John[5] > Wealthy[6]   0 < 2 < 2h
Turner: Humphrey[1] > John[2] > Ruth[3]   3 < 3e

Watson: Robert[1](+Elizabeth -?-) > George[2] > Phebe[3]   3g
White: Joseph[1] > Ann[2]   2
Winslow: John[1] > Susanna[2]   4 < 4e
Woods: Abigail   2

Young: Jane

Appendix D
Census Schedules and Other Records for
Adriana Porter and her Family

In this appendix we give the data for Adriana Porter and her parents and for her brother and his family from the Canadian Census for 1881, taken from the Mormon on-line genealogical resource <www.familysearch.org>.

We next give the data for Adriana Porter and her family from the United States Census for 1900, 1910, 1920, and 1930, transcribed from the images on line at <www.genealogy.com> and <www.ancestry.com>.

We also give abstracts of certain other records that have been found for Adriana Porter and her family, taken from different sources.

1881 Canadian Census Entry
for Henry Porter and Family

Yarmouth, Yarmouth County, Nova Scotia

Household 286

Name	Marital Status	Gender	Ethnic Origin	Age	Birth-place	Occupation	Religion
Henry Porter	M	M	English	60	N.S.*	Truckman	Baptist
Sarah Porter	M	F	English	62	N.S.	**	Baptist
Addie Porter	**	F	English	22	N.S.	Seamstress	Baptist

Household 287

Name	Marital Status	Gender	Ethnic Origin	Age	Birth-place	Occupation	Religion
William Porter	M	M	English	31	N.S.	Labourer	Baptist
Janet Porter	M	F	English	32	N.S.	**	Baptist
Wiletta Porter	**	F	English	14	N.S.	Student	Baptist
Clementina Porter	**	F	English	11	N.S.	Student	Baptist
Annie Porter	**	F	English	9	N.S.	Student	Baptist
Lennie Porter	**	F	English	7	N.S.	Student	Baptist

---

*N.S. = Nova Scotia; ** = no entry in this column

1900 United States Census Entry for William H. Healy and Family

State: Massachusetts
County: Suffolk
City: Boston (Roslindale)
E.D.: 1516
Page: 12A

Address: 6 South Water Street

1 House: 226
2 Family: 277

3	4	5	6	7	8	9	10	11	12	13	14	15	16	17	18	19	20	21	22	23	24	25	26	27	28
Healy, Wm H.	Hd	W	M	03/1857	43	M	11	*	*	CnE	CnE	CnE	1880	20	Pa	Contractor's Bookkeeper	0	*	Y	Y	Y	R	*	H	*
---, Addie	Wf	W	F	07/1857	42	M	11	1	1	CnE	CnE	CnE	1880	20	*	*	*	*	Y	Y	Y	*	*	*	*
---, Walter H.	Sn	W	M	07/1895	4	S	*	*	*	MA	CnE	CnE	*	*	*	*	*	*	*	*	*	*	*	*	*

Key to Columns

3   Name of Person
4   Relation to Head

Personal Description:
5   Color or Race
6   Sex
7   Date of Birth (Month / Year)
8   Age at Last Birthday
9   Single, Married, Widowed, or Divorced
10   Years Married
11   Children Born
12   Children Living

Place of Birth:
13   Person
14   Father
15   Mother

Citizenship:
16   Year of Immigration
17   Number of Years in U.S.
18   Naturalization

Occupation, Trade, or Profession:
19   Occupation
20   Months not Employed

Education:
21   Attended School (in Months)
22   Can Read
23   Can Write
24   Can Speak English

Ownership of Home:
25   Owned or Rented
26   Owned Free or Mortgaged
27   Farm or House
28   No. of Farm Schedule

Abbreviations

* = no entry in this column
4   Hd = head, Wf = wife, Sn = son
13-15   MA = Massachusetts, CnE = Canada (English)

1910 United States Census Entry for <u>William H. Healy and Family</u>

State: Massachusetts County: Middlesex City: Melrose E.D.: 947 Page: 3B

Address: 36 Gooch Street

1 House: 65
2 Family: 71

3	4	5	6	7	8	9	10	11	12	13	14	15	16	17	18	19	20	21	22	23	24	25	26	27	28	29	30	31	32
Healy, Wm H.	Hd	M	W	51	M	21	*	*	Cn/Eng	Cn/Eng	Cn/Eng	1878	Na	Eng	Bookkeeper	Construction Co.	W	No	0	Y	Y	*	R	*	H	*	*	*	*
----, Addie	Wf	F	W	52	M	21	1	1	Cn/Eng	Cn/Eng	Cn/Eng	1880	*	Eng	None	*	*	*	*	Y	Y	*	*	*	*	*	*	*	*
----, Walter E.	Sn	M	W	14	S	*	*	*	MA	Cn/Eng	Cn/Eng	*	*	Eng	None	*	*	*	*	Y	Y	Y	*	*	*	*	*	*	*

[Healy, W. H.]
[Healy, A.]
[Healy, W. E.]

Key to Columns

3 Name of Person
4 Relation to Head

Personal Description:
5 Sex
6 Color or Race
7 Age at Last Birthday
8 Single, Married, Widowed, or Divorced
9 Years in Present Marriage
10 Children Born
11 Children Living

Place of Birth and Mother Tongue:
12 Person
13 Father
14 Mother

Citizenship:
15 Year of Immigration
16 Naturalized or Alien
17 Able to Speak English or Other Language

Occupation:
18 Trade or Profession
19 Kind of Business
20 Employed or Working on Own Account

If an employee,
21 Whether Out of Work on April 15, 1910
22 Number of Weeks out of Work in 1909

Education:
23 Can Read
24 Can Write
25 Attended School since September 1, 1909

Ownership of Home:
26 Owned or Rented
27 Owned Free or Mortgaged
28 Farm or House
29 No. of Farm Schedule

Other:
30 Survivor of Union or Confederate Army or Navy
31 Blind (Both Eyes)
32 Deaf and Dumb

Abbreviations

* = no entry in this column
4 Hd = head, Wf = wife, Sn = son
12-14, 17 MA = Massachusetts, Cn = Canada, Eng = English

1920 United States Census Entry for <u>William H. Healy and Family</u>

State: Massachusetts County: Middlesex City: Melrose E.D.: 343 Page: 3A
1-2 Address: 76 First Street
3 House: 44
4 Family: 51

5	6	7	8	9	10	11	12	13	14	15	16	17	18	19	20	21	22	23	24	25	26	27	28	29
Healey, William H.	Hd	O	M	M	W	63	M	1876	Na	1881	*	Y	Y	Cn	En	Irl	En	Irl	En	Y	Agent	Insurance	W	*
----, Addie	Wf	*	*	F	W	63	M	1880	Na	1882	*	Y	Y	Cn	En	Cn	En	Cn	En	Y	none	*	*	*
----, Walter E.	Sn	*	*	M	W	24	S	*	*	*	*	Y	Y	MA	*	Cn	En	Cn	En	Y	Engineer	Leather Factory	*	*

Key to Columns

5 Name of Person
6 Relation to Head

Ownership of Home:
7 Owned or Rented
8 Owned Free or Mortgaged

Personal Description:
9 Sex
10 Color or Race
11 Age at Last Birthday
12 Single, Married, Widowed, or Divorced

Citizenship:
13 Year of Immigration
14 Naturalized or Alien
15 Year of Naturalization

Education:
16 Attended School since September 1, 1919
17 Can Read
18 Can Write

Place of Birth & Mother Tongue:
19-20 Person
21-22 Father
23-24 Mother
25 Able to Speak English

Occupation:
26 Trade or Profession
27 Kind of Business
28 Employed or Working on Own Account
29 No. of Farm Schedule

Abbreviations

* = no entry in this column
6 Hd = head, Wf = wife, Sn = son
19-24 MA = Massachusetts, Cn = Canada, Irl = Ireland, En = English

1930 United States Census Entry for <u>Walter E. Healy and Family</u>

State: Massachusetts   County: Middlesex   City: Melrose   E.D.: 9-348   Page: 11A

1-2 Address: 76 First Street
3 House: 240
4 Family: 268

5	6	7	8	9	10	11	12	13	14	15	16	17	18	19	20	21	22	23	24	25	26	27	28	29	30	31	32
Healy Walter E.	Hd	O	7000	N	*	M	W	34	M	29	N	Y	MA	CnE	CnE	*	*	*	Y	Painter	House	*	N	20	Y	WW	*
----, Ola	Wf	*	*	*	*	F	W	26	M	21	N	Y	CnE	CnE	CnE	Eng	1921	Al	Y	none	*	*	*	*	*	*	*
-----, Phyllis	Da	*	*	*	*	F	W	1.5	S	*	N	*	MA	MA	CnE	*	*	*	*	none	*	*	*	*	N	*	*
-----, William	Fa	*	*	*	*	M	W	72	M	31	N	Y	CnE	CnE	CnE	Eng	1870	Na	Y	Agent	Insurance	*	Y	*	N	*	*
-----, Addie	Mo	*	*	*	*	F	W	70	M	29	N	Y	CnE	CnE	CnE	Eng	1902	Na	Y	none	*	*	*	*	*	*	*

Key to Columns

5   Name of Person
6   Relation to Head

Ownership of Home:
7   Owned or Rented
8   Value if Owned;
    Monthly Rent if Rented
9   Radio Set
10   Lives on a Farm

Personal Description:
11   Sex
12   Color or Race
13   Age at Last Birthday
14   Single, Married, Widowed, or Divorced
15   Age at First Marriage

Education:
16   Attended School or College
    since September 1, 1929
17   Can Read and Write

Place of Birth:
18   Person
19   Father
20   Mother
21   Home Language before Coming to U.S.

Citizenship:
22   Year of Immigration
23   Naturalization
24   Able to Speak English

Occupation and Industry:
25   Occupation
26   Industry
27   Class of Worker

Employment:
28   Whether at Work Yesterday
    (or Last regular Working Day)
29   Unemployment Schedule No.

Veterans:
30   Whether a U.S. Veteran
31   Which War

Farm Schedule:
32   No. on Farm Schedule

Abbreviations

* = no entry in this column
6   Hd = head, Wf = wife, Da = daughter, Fa = father, Mo = mother
18-21   MA = Massachusetts, CnE = Canada English, Eng = English

Note: The age of Phyllis is given as 1 6/12. It is unclear whether her given name is spelled Phyllis or Phellis. The handwriting is so cramped that many letters and numbers are not quite clear.

From the Vital Records of Rhode Island, 1636-1930
(Online at <www.ancestry.com>)

Marriages:

Israel Porter and Lydia A. Magray	26 August 1867
Addie Porter and William H. Healy	24 April 1888
Lydia A. Porter and Bernard McLaughlin	5 July 1881

Births of the children of Jacob Israel Porter and Lydia Abigail Porter:

John F. Porter	27 May 1868
Charles W. Porter	6 May 1870
Lena E. Porter	29 November 1872
Frank A. Porter	15 October 1875
Grace F. Porter	?ca. 1878

Deaths of the children of Jacob Israel Porter and Lydia Abigail Porter:

John F. Porter	28 August 1870
Lena A. Porter	16 January 1875
Charles W. Porter	16 October 1925

[Presumably Frank A. Porter died after 1930, as his death is not recorded in this database. Nor is the death of Jacob Israel Porter recorded here, although the United States Census for 1880 lists his wife Lydia as a widow.]

Possible marriages of the children of Jacob Israel Porter and Lydia Abigail Porter:

Charles A. Porter and Hittle E. Crowell	26 May 1892
Frank E. Porter and Tjestke J. DeVries	14 June 1918

From the Indexes to the Vital Records at the Massachusetts State Archives

Birth Indexes:

Walter Ellsworth Healey [sic], 2 July 1985 at Plymouth (vol. 449, page 673, no. 98)

Marriage Indexes:

Walter E. Healy and Ola B. Turner, 1925 at Melrose (vol. 34, page 396)

Death Indexes

William Henry M. Healey [sic], 1927 at Melrose (vol. 47, page 118)
  [Is this an otherwise unknown child of Walter E. and Ola B. Healy?]

Walter Ellsworth Healey [sic], 1931 at Melrose (vol. 62, page 192)

Addie (Porter) Healy, 1946 at Melrose (vol. 62, p. 348)

[An entry for William H. Healy, who died in 1932, was not found.]

Abstracts of Death Certificates
at the Massachusetts State Archives

Death Certificates 1931, vol. 56, pg. 192

Name: Walter Ellsworth Healey [sic], 76 First St., Melrose
Died: 29 August 1931, aged 36y 1m 22d
Cause of death: Gas poisoning during World War [I]
Occupation: Painter (worked 3 years as such, until July 1926)
Born: Plymouth, Mass.
Father: William Henry Healey, born Windsor, N.S.
Mother: Addie Porter, born Yarmouth, N.S.
[Deduced birthday: 7 July 1895; actual birthday 2 July, 1895]

Death Certificates 1932, vol. 75, pg. 548

Name: Wm. Henry Healy, 76 First St., Melrose
Died: 10 May (injured 7 May) 1932, aged 75y 1m 23d, at Central Hospital, Somerville
Cause of death: Hit by motorcycle, fracturing of skull
Occupation: Insurance Broker (worked 15 years as such, until May 7, 1932)
Born: Windsor, N.S.
Father: Richard Healy, born - N.S.
Mother: Eliza J. Millitt, born - N.S.
[Deduced birthday: 17 March 1857; actual birthday in March 1857]

Death Certificates 1946, vol. 62, pg. 348

Name: Addie Healy (Porter), Fitch Home, 75 Lake Ave.
Died: 1 March 1946, aged 87y 7m 9d
Cause of death: Acute congestive [heart] failure, due to chronic myocarditis (25 years)
Occupation: At Home
Born: Yarmouth, N.S.
Father: Henry Porter, born Hebron, N.S.
Mother: Sarah Cook, born -, N.S.
[Informant was Jane E. Day, Matron, Fitch Home]
[Deduced birthday: 20 July 1858; actual birthday in July 1857]

Notices of Marriages and Deaths
from The Melrose Free Press

HEALY - TURNER

The marriage of Miss Ola B. Turner and Walter E. Healy, both of 76 First Street, took place April 16, Rev. Walter E. Woodbury, pastor of the First Baptist Church, officiating.

[Friday, April 24, 1925, p. 2]

WALTER E. HEALEY

Walter E. Healey, a World War veteran, died at his home, 76 First Street, last Saturday after a lingering illness. He was 36 years old, a native of Plymouth and had resided in Melrose 26 years. During the World War he served in the Headquarters Company, 55th Coast Artillery and was overseas more than a year. While in the service in France he was gassed and was disabled during the remainder of his life. He was a member of Melrose Post 90, American Legion. Surviving him are his wife, Mrs. Ola Healey, one daughter, Phyllis Ruth, and his parents, Mr. and Mrs. William Healey of this city.

Military honors were paid the late veteran at his funeral services on Tuesday afternoon in the Legion Bungalow. Officers of the Melrose Post, A. L. conducted their ritual. Rev. John L. Ivey, pastor of the Methodist Episcopal Church, officiated at the services, with numerous members of the Legion post and relatives and friends of the deceased attending. Burial was in Wyoming Cemetery and a firing squad sounded a volley at the grave. There were many beautiful flowers.

[Friday, September 4, 1931, p. 12]

WILLIAM H. HEALEY

William H. Healey of 76 First Street died at the Central Hospital, Somerville, Tuesday afternoon from injuries he received last Saturday when struck by a motor-cycle which collided with a truck and then caromed from that vehicle and hit Mr. Healey. He was removed to the hospital where it was found he had suffered a compound fracture of the right arm and head injuries.

155

Mr. Healey was an insurance broker in Boston for a number of years. He was 75 years old, a native of Windsor, N. S. and had lived in the United States half a century and in Melrose 26 years.

Surviving him are his wife, Mrs. Addie Healey, and three sisters.

Funeral services will take place Friday afternoon at 2:30 o'clock at Clark's funeral parlors, South High Street, and burial will be in Wyoming Cemetery.

[Thursday, May 12, 1932, p. 7]

MRS. WILLIAM H. HEALY

Mrs. Addie (Porter) Healy, 87, widow of William Henry Healy, died on March 1, at the Fitch Home.

She had been a resident of this city for half a century, and for many years was an active member of the Legion Auxiliary, the Grange, Rebekaha, and the Relief Corps.

A granddaughter, Phyllis Healy, 84 Cottage Street, is the only survivor.

Funeral services were held on March 4, at the home and conducted by the Rev. John L. Cairns. Burial was at Wyoming Cemetery.

[Thursday, March 14, 1946, p. 13]

[NB Rev. Cairns was 'present pastor of the First Methodist Church' according to the preceding obituary on that page.]

Abstract of William H. Healy's Naturalization Petition

Sworn in the Third District Court of Eastern Middlesex Co., Holden at Cambridge, Massachusetts (Deposited at the United States Archives, Waltham, Massachusetts)

Name:	William H. Healy
Occupation:	Civil Engineer
Residence:	32 Magazchu [= Massachusetts?], Cambridge
Born:	Windsor, Nova Scotia, 17 March 1857
Emigrated from:	Windsor, Nova Scotia
Emigrated to:	Watertown, Maine,
Date of Emigration:	15 October 1878
Date of this Petition:	17 November 1902
Primary Declaration:	District Court of East Norfolk, 1 July 1893

Social Security Death Index

(Online at <www.rootsweb.com>)

Chester D. Stetson, 26 August 1905 - 16 July 1993
Ola B. Stetson, 5 May 1903 - January 1996
Last residence of each at North Haven, New Haven County, Connecticut

Massachusetts Death Index

(Online at <www.ancestry.com>)

Ola Stetson, 5 May 1903 - 10 January 1996, died at Stoneham, Massachusetts

Transcription of Gravestones in Wyoming Cemetery, Melrose (Lot 400, Section 2)

```
1857      WILLIAM H.      1932

              HIS WIFE
    1857      ADDIE      1946

             THEIR SON
    1895      WALTER E.      1931

               HEALY
```

```
                +

             WALTER E.
              HEALY
                —
           MASSACHUSETTS
                —
            PVT. 53 REGT.
             COAST ART.
           AUGUST 29, 1931
```

Appendix E
The First Two Publications of
the *Rede of the Wiccae*

In this appendix we give an accurate transcription of Gwen Thomson's entire article, "Wiccan-Pagan Potpourri," as it appeared in issue #69 of *Green Egg* (for Ostara 1975). This contains her definitive published text of the *Rede of the Wiccae.* We also give an accurate transcription of the similar, but distorted text of the Rede as it was published a year earlier, in *Earth Religion News,* volume 3, issue 1 (for the Spring Equinox, 1974), page 3. This is the only appearance of the *Rede* in print before Gwen's own article. (Since Gwen refers to this earlier publication in her *Green Egg* article, the reader may wish to see it for himself or herself.)

Wiccan-Pagan Potpourri*
by Lady Gwen[1]

A Fundamentalist Christian recently said to me, "Satan rules this planet!" I replied: "I know it!" My answer was unnerving to the person making the statement due to the fact that the Fundamentalists, along with numerous other Christian denominations, firmly believe that Witches and Pagans are "devil-worshipers." I did not elaborate upon the fact that we do not believe in a "devil" as such, but we *do* believe in a *controlling force* that is anathema to our way of life as we would like to live it, and should be able to live it, upon this planet. Our ancient lore tells us that thousands of years ago there were two forces seeking control of the mode of life upon this planet; one group wishing to teach mankind the "facts of life" and the other wishing to exploit mankind. There were many names applied to these beings: Gods, angels, Watchers, sons of God, etc. The leaders of these two opposing forces, for want of a better term or name, were referred to as The Lord of Light and The Lord of Darkness. There is no need to be specific about which of them wanted what. Oh yes, and lest we forget . . . their "hosts" (in modern terminology, armies).

The Christian *Bible,* garbled as it currently is, speaks of a battle in the "heavens" . . . well, we know there was one, although the Christians have their space-time continuum a bit mixed up . . . to the point where it is all done and over with, according to them. But, we know that as it was in the beginning so it will be in the end . . . giving us the Alpha and Omega of history. When Christians speak of "fallen angels" and "salvation," I merely reply, "Ummmm . . . of course." Then they are gently felled with the statement, "If the Lord of *Light* lost the battle for control of earth . . . who *won*?" They were taught that the Lord of Light was Lucifer, a very naughty angel who went against God and got his. Along with his followers, naturally. It is clear that a large number of the followers of the Lord of Light were confined to Earth, bred with Earth people and produced what we now have as a breed of "different" beings, classified as people who "have the *power*" or "*knowing ones*." Thus, we have an admixture upon this planet of Light and Darkness. The demarcation line becomes more obvious daily. Shall we call it "The Omega Caper?"

When it comes down to the nitty gritty of hassles and bickering and the rest of the fertilizer . . . consider the fact that antagonistic elements of Darkness infiltrate for the express purpose of dimming the *light*. The sad tales of recorded history are replete with data on thousands of enlightened ones who brought forth progress upon the earth as new inventions and new ways of thought in order to *advance* mankind. Were they not all ridiculed at one time or another? Was there not an element among

---

*Excerpted from *Green Egg,* issue #69 (for Ostara 1975), pages 9-11.

mankind that continually sought to *prevent* progress? We have had our "Mighty Ones" who overcame the opposing and controlling forces to progress our people in spite of any obstacle . . . often at great personal sacrifice.

We are all well aware of the people who have been continuously opposed to our space program . . . they give various and sundry reasons: "expensive" (so what?); "we need the money for the poor and the needy;" or "we should not mess around with God's universe," etc., etc., blah, blah, blah. The numerous wars, inspired by Darkness, were also "expensive" . . . *very* expensive. The "poor and needy" wouldn't be about to get any of the lucre, and as for "God's universe" . . . it belongs to everyone to share equally. There is no need to be imprisoned upon the giant spaceship earth if one wishes to go elsewhere. For those who are not already well aware of it . . . the battle is once more raging. This time, however, the thumb-screws are on the other pinkies.

Old Religionists who allow themselves to be photographed by the news media in the "altogether" (sky-clad), and often in positions that suggest obscene practices, are not doing the Old Religion any service whatsoever, but rather giving it a very black eye. Worship in such a case, if it *is* worship, should be sacred to the Goddess and God alone and not for eyes of cowans to see and misinterpret. We live in a clothed society which is not all that ready to accept what *some* Witches or Pagans do. If we wish to get across the message that we are intelligent, dignified, and worthy of respect . . . just as much as the controlling religions of earth . . . then we should not use back-door tactics, but use some of the Wisdom our forebears bestowed upon us to give the proper impression of what and who we really are.

Many Witches ignore the age-old counseling of the Wise Ones as given in the *Rede.* **[9/10]** Many different traditions have different redes. That is understandable, considering the time involved from Alpha to Omega. Our own particular *Rede,* however, has appeared within the last year in a perverted form. That is to say, the wording has been changed.[2] This is sad for those who are seeking the Light of the Old Religion, because it confuses them. The same thing was done to the ancient seals of Solomon, and thus we do not have his great wisdom as it was meant to be in the original form. Some would-be artists thought to "improve" upon the drawings of the seals, not realizing it was not artwork, but sacred symbolism . . . not to be tampered with. Thus, many wonder why the current seals so often bring them undesired results or no results at all.

We are not "into" Cabalistic magic, as such, but do not deny its relationship to our way of life. We have all received our lore from the same root source. As a Traditionalist, versed in lore taken from certain Witches of the British Isles, I can say that our own particular tradition consisted of the practices and beliefs of folk Witches and not those people who were generally wealthy enough to be formally

161

educated. Country people were simple people and had simple rituals in practice and wording. Many never knew how to read or write, but they were not without their share of "nobles" who did know how. Many Old Religion dances and songs became the nursery rhymes and dances of children, following the centuries-old "Witch" trials. Thus, many legends and songs are almost child-like in their context . . . because this was the level of basic understanding of folk Witches at that time. Unable to openly express what they knew to be *truth* in actual "university" terms . . . they resorted to simple symbolism in ritual, legend, and drawings, and preserved their sacred heritage in the most comprehensive manner, and in a manner that would be ignored by their adversaries, for the most part. Our own particular form of the Wiccan *Rede* is that which was passed on to her heirs by Adriana Porter, who was well into her nineties when she crossed over into the Summerland in the year 1946. This *Rede* in its original form is as follows.

Rede of the Wiccae
(Being knowne as the counsel of the Wise Ones)

1. Bide the Wiccan laws ye must
   in perfect love an perfect trust.

2. Live an let live -
   fairly take an fairly give.

3. Cast the Circle thrice about
   to keep all evil spirits out.

4. To bind the spell every time,
   let the spell be spake in rhyme.

5. Soft of eye an light of touch -
   speak little, listen much.

6. Deosil go by the waxing Moon -
   sing an dance the Wiccan rune.

7. Widdershins go when the Moon doth wane,
   an the Werewolf howls by the dread Wolfsbane.

8. When the Lady's Moon is new,
   kiss the hand to her times two.

9. When the Moon rides at her peak,
   then your heart's desire seek.

10. Heed the Northwind's mighty gale -
    lock the door and drop the sail.

11. When the wind comes from the South,
    love will kiss thee on the mouth.

12. When the wind blows from the East,
    expect the new and set the feast.

13. When the West wind blows o'er thee,
    departed spirits restless be.

14. Nine woods in the Cauldron go -
    burn them quick an burn them slow.

15. Elder be ye Lady's tree -
    burn it not or cursed ye'll be.

16. When the Wheel begins to turn -
    let the Beltane fires burn.

17. When the Wheel has turned a Yule,
    light the Log an let Pan rule.

18. Heed ye flower, bush an tree -
    by the Lady blessed be.

19. Where the rippling waters go,
    cast a stone an truth ye'll know.

20. When ye have need,
    hearken not to other's greed.

21. With the fool no season spend
    or be counted as his friend.

22. Merry meet an merry part -
    bright the cheeks an warm the heart.

23. Mind the Threefold Law ye should -
    three times bad an three times good.

24. When misfortune is enow,
    wear the blue star on thy brow.

25. True in love ever be
    unless thy lover's false to thee.

26. Eight words the Wiccan Rede fulfill -
    an it harm none, do what ye will.

The foregoing is explained fully to the initiated Witch. The contents of the *Book of Shadows* (our public name for it) must be orally taught as well as copied. All wording has its special meaning which the Wise can often quickly discern. Meditation is a most important adjunct to the learning of the Mysteries of the Old Religion. The number of Old Religionists currently abiding by the counsel of the Wise can be counted on the fingers of one hand and the thumb would be left over.

There is only one form of wisdom that time alone can bestow, and that is lessons **[10/11]** learned from *experience.* Our children were taught to respect the old ones, even though they were often people of little formal education or very simple in their ways. They had lived long and had, therefore, experienced much of life and its ways. Their advice through *their own* lessons learned was considered invaluable, and thus they were held in deep respect for those things in which they had learned Wisdom. Children were not taught to strive for perfection, but for Wisdom. Perfection is a broad concept with different meanings for different people. It actually does not exist. The caution was, "Do not seek perfection in others unless you yourself can give it." Therefore . . . we have the counsel to "live an let live . . . "

When anyone refers to a particular Old Religion tradition as a "sect" it brings to mind bug spray. It is a poor term to apply to a sacred way of life, and the word "cult" is enough to set one's teeth on edge. Although *Webster's* now gives it a more dignified connotation, the general public and *Webster* do not necessarily agree on all points of definition. There was originally just a single tradition of Witchcraft and many traditions within Paganism due to country, customs, etc. When certain priests of the early Christian church became bored with their celibate life they perverted their own religion by reversing their rituals and brought forth Satanism. Why they insisted upon calling themselves Witches is anyone's guess, for the majority of them still do it. Unless, perhaps, they are so guilt ridden about their practices and beliefs that they wish to place the blame elsewhere. Genuine Witches and Pagans are not running around cutting off the heads of black chickens, nor are they offering up babies and virgins to some obscure demon. We have too much respect for life. It is almost useless to try getting the truth across to those who do not and will not understand our ways due to a messed-up news media and the general Christian-Judeo clamor for titillating reading . . . such as evidenced in the book, *The Devil on Lammas Night* by Susan Howatch, whoever that is. It is a cross-continent version of what the adversary imagines Witchcraft to be or would like the reading public to think it is. A quite exciting and well-written book, to be sure. An accursed lie, however. How unlike the beautiful writing of Mary Stewart, the author of the much-read and beloved book, *The Crystal Cave,* and its sequel, *The Hollow Hills.* Mary Stewart is to Susan Howatch what diamonds are to coal.

At this point I should like to quote from a very learned patriarch of the Old Religion . . . one whom we would refer to as a "Wizen Elder" in our tradition. (Wizen being pronounced as "whizzen." It is derived from the title Wizard . . . one highly skilled in the arts of the Craft.) I feel he would not mind my including his comments on book authors at this point. They are simply stated, "The Craft view is that a book is only a man talking on paper and is no more accurate than the spoken word by the same man. Any man who talks for an extended length of time must make a few mistakes. No book, therefore, not even a college text, is 100 percent accurate. Also, no man has all the facts about any particular subject. There is always something more to be told . . . something the author did not know." I might only add that this applies to female authors as well. " . . . speak little, listen much . . . "

Many in the Old Religion are now finding it wise to shun the limelight and keep their activities secret from the public on all levels. One might even say they are going "underground." This includes many High Priestesses and High Priests who are either choosing to take their entire Covens "underground" or to practice their religion quietly by themselves. This is logical and sane at this time in history. It does not mean a creeping away into some hidden corner for fear of the foe, but a carefully calculated plan to keep the foe guessing. Considering the apparent IQ level of many of our critics, the cerebral exercise will do them good. Our forebears did not go about thumping their chests and proclaiming to the world at large "I am a Witch!" simply because it was the "in" thing or the current social "fad." They did not wish to raise eyebrows or attract the adversary or the ever-increasing horde of misfits. In discretion and Wisdom they preserved the old truths . . . . else we would not have them today.

Food for thought—I don't care what anyone does just so long as they do not interfere with Life, this planet, or me. Surprising how limiting this can be. "As you sow . . . so shall you reap" is not a Christian original . . . it is the Threefold Law simply expressed in farm language. Disharmony begets disharmony and time travels in a *circle*, not a straight line. The serpent eating his own tail. Perversions of ancient traditions often bring ancient curses as well. The invisible becomes manifest. Twin earths exchanging bric-a-brac. The insatiable guru-chasers, book collectors, coven hoppers, name-droppers, and ego-trippers. We've all had our share of them. Monsters roam the planet in various guises. People who seldom make anyone happy . . . feigning Wisdom. Nobody can hear a whisper while they're talking. Wiccan-Pagan teachings are not for everyone.

The Wiccan *Rede**

Bide the Wiccan Rede laws ye must, in perfect love and perfect trust
Live and let live, fairly take and fairly give
Cast the circle thrice about to keep all evil spirits out.
To bind the spell everytime, let the spell be spoken in rhyme
Soft of eye and light of touch, speak little and listen much
Deosil go by waxing moon, chanting out the Wiccan rune
Widdershins go by waning moon, chanting out the baneful rune
When the Lady's moon is new, kiss the hand to her times two
When the moon rides at her peak, then your heart's desire seek
Heed the north wind's mighty gale, lock the door and drop the sail
When the wind comes from the South, love will kiss thee on the mouth
When the moor wind blows from the West, departed spirits have no rest
When the wind blows from the East, expect the new and set the feast
Nine woods in the cauldron go, burn them quick and burn them slow
Elder be Ye Lady's tree, burn it not or cursed you'll be
When the wheel begins to turn, let the Beltane fires burn
When the wheel has turned a Yule, light the log and the Horned One rules
Heed ye flower, bush and tree, by the Lady Blessed Be
Where the rippling waters go, cast a stone and truth you'll know
When ye have need, harken not to others' greed
With a fool no season spend, or be counted as his friend
Merry meet and merry part, bright the cheeks and warm the heart
Mind the threefold Law ye should, three times bad and three times good
When misfortune is enow, wear the blue star upon thy brow
True in love ever be, unless thy lover's false to thee
Eight words the Wiccan Rede fulfill—an ye harm none, do what ye will

*Excerpted from *Earth Religion News* 1/3 (Spring Equinox,1974): 3.

Endnotes

1. The editors of *Green Egg* gave the byline as "by Lady Gwen, Welsh Tradition Wicca," with a tag of their own devising. The tag is not Gwen's, she did not call her Tradition Welsh or find the label acceptable. She wrote to the editors of *Green Egg* in protest soon after issue #69 appeared, and the editors printed her letter with an apology in issue #71 (for Litha 1975), p. 39. A subsequent letter and apology appeared in issue #72 (for Lughnnasad 1975), p. 44-5. The first paragraph of Gwen's letter says, "May I inquire what enterprising individual added "Welsh Traditional Wicca" to my name in an article I wrote many months ago entitled "Wiccan-Pagan Potpourri" and which appeared in *Osttara GE* 69? For the record, we are not Welsh. I do believe we ran this route a few years ago, and it seems that once more clarification is needed. We are and always have been simply Traditionalists. We use the term Celtic Traditionalist to differentiate us from the ones who claim to be Welsh, and I know of only one tradition that has the right to use that name. If there are others, I do not know of them. My apologies, but we are not Welsh. We prefer to be simply known as "Traditionalists." [The "ones who claim to be Welsh" included Ed Buczynski, who planned to call his coven (as Gwen wrote in a private letter to the founding High Priestess of another tradition) the "New York Coven of Brythonic-Welsh Traditionalist Witches." See page 54.]

2. This refers to the 1974 publication in *Earth Religion News,* which almost certainly derives from Ed Buczynski's text. See page 166 for the text and page 54 for the background information.